Nietzsche
and Ikeda

맑은샘

Table of contents

Prologue

Section 1 About Nietzscheanism

Section 2 Nietzscheanism is completed by SGI this way

Ubermensch and Buddha nature

Nietzsche wrote in his major work, 「Thus Spoke Zarathustra」 that "Every god is dead. Now we want Ubermensch to appear. Ubermensch is the meaning of this earth." Ubermensch that he mentioned means the most ideal human life, which can be expressed as the 'eternal positive song by the healthy person'.

Furthermore, Nietzsche said "I want people to understand their existence's meaning. It is Ubermensch, and the lightning striking penetrating dark clouds-human" Also he said, "Humans are the rope between Ubermensch and the animal, the one rope hanging over the abyss."

The story became long, but to summarize in short the Nietzscheanism, would it like this?

"Human should not borrow the power of the god, but when

human call the 'will of the power' inside their inner side by him/herself, which is Ubermensch, and live like 'Ubermensch styled life', and then finally liberal spirit can be acquired and furthermore live 'the life as a master'. This is the happy life human chases."

The Ubermensch Nietzsche called is Buddha nature written in Lotus Sutra, essence of the Mahayana Buddhism. Buddha nature means 'Universal life force' with infinite life force, wisdom, mercy and supporting every living thing. Also, Buddhism explains that this 'living force' exists within human of course, and every life alive in the world.

Live is the actively moving force and abundance itself. In this actively moving force and abundance, life affirms itself and the world. We feel the liveliness, vigor, and refreshed from life, and we experience joy and wonder from abundance. The life in this context like soaring spring water.

The most important thing in the world is the life of one human, which is taught as the life, Buddha nature(Ubermensch) prepared within one human's life. Lotus Sutra which want it to be called and enter the Nirvana in the present's life, and the Nietzsche who describes the 'heart of Lotus Sutra' with the elegant style of writing, philosophically and literary boldly fancy and beautiful. These two doesn't seem to be related at all, but the message of "You, live the master of your life" is perfectly identical even it can be described mysterious.

Nietzsche endlessly wrote his conviction in his writings without being tired. Among his numerous writings, the following expression is the most standing out among many flowers like it represents his philosophy. What is the reason?

"Look, I teach you the Ubermensch! Ubermensch is the meaning of this earth. Let your will to tell. That Ubermensch should be the meaning of the earth! Brothers, swear to be faithful to the earth."

What does the Nietzscheanism insist? Isn't it life as a master through 'revolution of human nature', which is the 'human revolution'! Wasn't he the person who tried to change human history, which can only be called tragic, with considerable effort through his philosophy and idea? Isn't Nietzsche should at least be assessed as like that?

When he finished the writing of 『Thus Spoke Zarathustra』, Nietzsche left this expression soothing his mind of sadness as "My time didn't come yet. Let's wait 100 years. When we meet the great noon, I hope one genius who can understand human very well to appear and excavate the person named Nietzsche from the grave and flower my philosophy and idea."

Time flies and everything changes. The present period of us is the 100 year of Nietzche told, and 'the great noon' of his prophecy is being received by our mankind. By the way furthermore the great genius Nietzsche longed for has already emerged and proved the greatness of his philosophy.

The great noon means the period of shortest shadow, which is the period of rising of 'the Sun of Hope' making a dark cloud out and illusion shortest. 'The sun of hope' means the Buddhist writings of 'three thousand realms in a single moment of life(一念三千) of Lotus Sutra' which taught one human's possibility and nobility to the limit, which is that one brilliant flame rises on the Latter Days of the Law, brightening surroundings, lightening up the world.

The Latter Days of the Law can be described in short as the period of the crisis when Buddhist law or society meet the dead-end and if they were left without care, the chaos and disintegration cannot but to come. It is so-called as the degeneration age.

Many people don't know yet, to tell you the truth, Nietzscheanism has already flowered as countless fancy flowers here and there in the name of 'Soka Renaissance', and it is flowering now also.

If the core of the Nietzscheanism is the Free spirit through 'the Human Revolution' which means the master of the life should be human, and acquiring that mind to finish the 'Human Revolution', there are people who flower his philosophy as the 'practice of life' in the reality's hard life.

Astonishingly people who flower the Nietzscheanism are the members of SGI(Soka Gakkai International), and the Daisaku Ikeda; 3rd President, who is leading the organization is in the center.

SGI is lay Buddhist organization approved devotee's organization which honors Lotus Sutra as the principal icon of the faith.

The event of meeting Nietzscheanism by Charles Lee(the name of the author) was such a coincidence. saw on one evening unconsciously by Youtube. For him who deemed himself as just a good believer, the philosophy was just luxurious amusement of the idea.

Karl Marks once told.

"Philosophers just interprets the world differently. Now the important thing is to revolutionize the world. Through action rather than theory."

Philosophy is the study of realizing the logic of the matter through the deep reasoning, and realization through that study gets lost with time goes on like "Things get by the reason is to be lost when time flies". However, the thing experienced by oneself cannot be easily lost. To explain it, for the realization got through the philosophy to contribute to the human lives, when appearing as the 'power of belief' through the repetitive everyday life's practice, that realization can throw the light to us. 'The power of the belief' means that already we entered into the world of religion.

I think Marks who already knew that the true limit of the philosophy more than any other else.

Arnold Toynbee told like this.

"The modern threat to the human survival can be eliminated only by the revolutionary change inside one and one person's mind, and to make the willpower to practice the ideal, this revolution of the mind should be developed, I think, through the religion."

Nietzsche also said, "Philosophy should service to human and human life. The value of the philosophy is in increasing creative possibility and making life positive. When philosophy doesn't lead to the practice of life, what value does it base on?"

The reason of Charles Lee's having interest in the Nietzscheanism was 2 reasons. Firstly, the expression of Nietzsche "When philosophy doesn't lead to the practice of life, what value does it base on?". How Nietzsche can increase his philosophy to the practice of life! And does it mean that he had the ground-breaking 'performance method' that making us astonishing, to which everyone cannot but to admit, which makes any general person can be superhuman?

If then, what is the secret of the enlightening! And the second reason was that Nietzscheanism was similar to the Buddhism very much. Buddhism is a life philosophy which told about the mystic mystery of life. Nietzscheanism is also a life philosophy calling life force, that is Ubermensch. His philosophy is very similar to Lotus Sutra, which is called as the essence of the Buddhism. In some way the two has so many similarities, I think Nietzsche described Lotus Sutra literary in his brilliant and fancy style of the writing.

Nietzsche is called as the philosopher of life. People say, to him, life was philosophy itself, and his philosophy was the life itself. Also, it deemed by himself, to the Charles Lee who lives as SGI member, the life was his religion, and his religion was his life.

People tend to classify the 'secular world' and the 'world of belief', and it is wrong, Charles Lee shaking his head to no. For him, the belief is the light which gives the light of hope to the secular life which is can be easily dull. The religious faith is the source of the vitality which leads the track of the society and human life to the hoped direction.

Charles Lee's life goal was to finish the 'Human Revolution' that is, to enter Nirvana based on Lotus Sutra which told about the mystery of life. He advanced to the place, to climb up to the apex. In no time 30 years had passed, and in result, he lived his life becoming the superhuman, the Ubermensch which is mentioned by the Nietzsche.

There was no special reason for Charles Lee's living his life this way. He didn't want to be an ideal or standing out person at all. He just has lived his 'way of human' laid in front of him. It is because there were no other ways but to that way.

Although human beings cannot see, there is a bird-flying path in the air, and there is a way for fish to swim in the great sea. Just like him, there is a way for humans to shine on themselves.

The path means living in harmony with the great universe's life, that is, the marvelous law of Buddha. It is to be with the laws and rhythms of the universe as if the sun were sending light to resuscitate life, as the moonlight gently touches it.

"The laws of the universe are inherent in human life. Only when we realize this, we can trust our power."

This is the word of Tagore, a great poet of India.

Charles Lee is not sure where he is located of "the way of the entering Nirvana." But I know one obvious fact. It's the way he's walked, and he calls it the Golden Way.

SGI President Ikeda says.

"Religion is meaningful of giving value to human life. Even if you can't see it, if it's idea and spirit is connected to the happiness forming in real society, it doesn't mean anything. The fundamental purpose of religion is to raise useful people.

What does religion exist for? It's for people's happiness. It's for a fruitful life. And in order to achieve that, we have to create a society that respects humans, and we have to cultivate a diverse human culture. In other words, when religion became the power to build a society, it was only then that religion achieved its purpose.

Faith is light. People who are full of strong beliefs are filled with light. Life shines through the light. Those who have unshakable conviction can enjoy happiness, like the moon shining in the dark night sky, like the sun dazzlingly shining in the bright daylight.

Human life is the continuation of change. Nothing happened until yesterday, but today we're at a crossroads where we have to make a decision, and from that moment on, we start changing for better or for worse. What gives us strength in this sea of change is a guide to the right path to the future, and a word of encouragement to revive us. Especially when you're standing in the middle of adversity.

The idea that religion is not scientific or necessary is main stream among today's intellectuals, but it is a misconception. Einstein, a great scientist, also argues the need for religion and says in his book. Also the literary giant Tolstoy said, "One of the most savage superstitions is the dogma that so-called modern scholars have, that humans can live without faith." in the 「A calendar of wisdom」. William Adams, an American writer in the 19th century, said, "Trust is an extension of reason."

When you get a cold grasp of life and social phenomena and

solve the agony of life, and figure out what life is and what the fundamental power of the universe is, you'll end up in religion."

Times change. And religion changes.

Religion is changing to take root in human life as the human emerges as the main character. Religion is getting closer to human life, drawing brilliant philosophies into life practice. It seems that Nietzsche, the king of philosophy, and Lotus Sutra, the highest peak of the religious world, meet and shake hands with each other.

The 21st century is called the "century of life." It means that a spring day has finally arrived in human history. And the brilliant, warm spring light focuses on the individual life that should be respected. It allows us to say that we were born into this world to make our life that we want, like the birth of the single flower is to show its beauty to the world.

Renaissance that sang the greatness of humanity. Many years have passed since it. So, since some time ago, we have waited anxiously for the revival of human nature in the human mind, and the "Soka Renaissance," which can be said to be the latter part of the Renaissance, is finally showing itself to the human world with the flag of a grasshopper.

Nietzsche's philosophy of voice, which has been spreading for thousands of years, is rising even higher and is flapping flags. His mature philosophy is resonating with the prelude to the great religious revolution of the Soka Renaissance.

But what about humans?

This book to be read is about Nietzsche's philosophy reflected in the eyes of a Buddhist (SGI member), his personal thought and opinions regarding the 'Human Revolution' the core subject among them, "You, live the master of your life!", and the stories about SGI President Ikeda.

About Nietzscheanism

Part 1

———

Bless this cup!
Full of golden water

Nietzsche's major and representative book, 「Thus Spoke Zarathustra」 was proudly included in the world literature complete collection being called as the flower of the modern philosophy, and it begins like this.

"By the time he became thirty, Zarathustra left the lakes of his hometown and home and went into the mountains. Here he lived ten years without being tired enjoying his spirit and solitude. But finally, a change of mind occurred. One morning at dawn, he rose from his seat and walked to the front of the sun. And said to the sun like this.

"You, great star! If you have no one to accept the light,

even if you shine the light, what is your happiness!

For the last ten years, you have risen here to my cave. But without me and my eagle and my snake, you would have finally hated your light and the path of the light.

We have waited for you every morning, and have blessed you in return for the fullness we get from you.

Behold! I am tired of my wisdom, like a bee which has gathered so much honey. Therefore, now I wish I had hands reaching out to me.

I'm going to give and distribute. Until the wise among human rejoices their stupidity, and the poor rejoice their fullness.

To do that, I have to go down to that abyss. Like you, falling to the other side of the sea and reflect the summer every evening. You overflowing star!

I must fall as you. Like the people I'm going to meet down there will say.

So bless me. You silent eyes! You who can see even great happiness without jealousy!

Bless this glass that is about to overflow! A glass out of which golden water flowing and to lighten up your joy to the whole world!

Look! I hope this glass is to be emptied again.

Zarathustra wants to be human again."

In this way, the fall of Zarathustra begun.

There are many philosophies in the world. Nietzsche's philosophy stands out in it. Why does it stand out? That's because he's telling us 'the active power of life'. The power of life unknowingly approaches us with the joy and hope of life. That's why Nietzsche philosophy is being loved by and attracting many people.

And there's another reason. That is, every philosophy existing in the world is only within the categories of Sravaka boundary or Pratyeka boundary. Sravaka boundary means literally the boundary of being enlightened by the others' teaching, and the Pratyeka boundary means the boundary of enlightenment by themselves through some objects, that is getting enlightenment independently.

Surprisingly, however, Nietzsche's mature philosophy portrays the boundary of the Buddha, the world's highest boundary that humans can reach.

The boundary of Buddha means the boundary of the enlightened who gives love and mercy to mankind showing the enlightenment on their body with realizing the eternal Law of Universe and Life. And any human who enters into the boundary of the Buddha, that life's every moment changes into the absolute respect and affection of happiness with supreme delight.

Nietzsche describes the mysterious world he has realized philosophically and literary through his brilliant and fancy style of writing. His heart, full of love and compassion, becomes his elegant and refined writing and comes close to us.

Because the boundary of the Buddha is very difficult to show it as it is the mysterious life and environment. This is why Nietzsche used countless parodies and metaphors in his works.

In Nietzsche's last work, "Ecce homo" Nietzsche said, "When Dr. Heinrich von Stein honestly complained once that I couldn't understand a word of my Zarathustra, I told him it was natural."

No wonder Nietzscheanism stands out among many philosophies. That's because the size and quality of the light sent to human life are different.

Nietzscheanism is abstruse, ambiguous, and hard to understand. But for some reason, It attracts my mind. It is even attractive. Is it possible that people are paying attention to Nietzscheanism because when they read his book, they somehow sympathize with his philosophy and ideas and feels a connection to the Nietzsche mysteriously? If so, the reason can be that the reader's heart contains the boundary of the Buddha in which Nietzsche lives.

We, human, left the Buddha nature, the best life which exists in one's inner side sleeping for a too long time in the dark and deep place. No, we even forgot if there was Buddha nature or not. The Buddha nature which is losing power on and on because the master do not call it and the Buddha nature losing its color and light in the barren and dry human world, Nietzsche approaches yelling to us in the voice of his soul without being tired to make the Buddha nature realize and to call it.

"Oh, should I be the light! The desire for something like night! Loneliness! The night has come. Passion rises from me now like spring water. The desire to tell someone.

Ah, the solitude of all the benefactors! Ah, the silence of all who shine! The night has come. Ah, should I be the light!

Ah, the misery of all the benefactors! Ah, my solar eclipse! Ah, a struggle for longing! Ah, a terrible hunger in satiety!

Now all the rising spring water speaks louder. My soul is also one of the rising fountains. Night has come. Only now do all the songs of the loved ones awaken. My soul is also the song of a person of love. The night has come. Ah, should I be the light!"

SGI President Ikeda says.

"Happiness ultimately depends on how determined you can be. Happiness is not in appearance or vanity. It just depends on how you feel. It's a deep resonance of life. It depends on the pleasant feeling of being rewarding every day and the deep satisfaction that comes from the sense of responsibility for the mission. People who feel this way are happy.

Without feeling the purpose and value of life, life is lonely and solitude without knowing why you were born as a human. Without any energy. Life without purpose cannot but to be seemed as the animal world.

Reversely, if we live for other people and society, and for ourselves, creating something and contributing, this life is the true life of satisfaction of hope. This is the life of Nietzsche's Ubermensch style of living. It is the best happiness and the life of the best fullness permitted for the human.

It's been a long time since the idea of 'grace' was forgotten in modern society. But humans cannot live alone. They live under the support of their parents, teachers, and human society. The human way is to realize it and to repay it with gratitude.

Teaching it is the Buddhism.

When we realize the sublime meaning of life, the infinite power inherent in life rises. And Buddha nature, which is also Ubermensch, allows us to say this. "The completion of human beings is achieved by getting caught in the heavy waves in the rough, rough seas of human beings and exploring the course of their faith to the end."

Buddhism teaches that every human being is a noble 'Buddha' by nature and that everyone has the right to be equal and happy. In other words, it is the humanism philosophy for peace and equality. And it is the Buddhism to teach how to use mercy, wisdom, and vitality of 'Buddha'.

The boundary of the Buddha is no other than Ubermensch or the state of life in which Buddha nature rises vigorously from its own life and shines its own life brightly. It's the affluence of life itself."

Nietzsche talks tirelessly.

"Dear you! I hope you will call your Buddha nature and lead an Ubermensch life. I hope to grow up to be superhuman. I want you to be strong."

And he says again.

"I gave mankind the biggest gift ever, the largest of all. With a voice that will spread for thousands of years, the book is the best and most profound book that exists in the world and was born from the deepest treasure house of truth. If I use the bucket to get it, the bucket becomes full of the wisdom of gold. This book is a gospel that makes a man happy and a future Bible that delivers joy. People must have the bravest fists with the softest fingers to own my book. You shouldn't have a small defect in your mind."

So here's a brief description of human life to help readers explore the Nietzscheanism.

There are ten worlds in human life. It is called the 'Ten Worlds' Life'. The ten worlds touch each other at every moment, causing a change often. The transformative actions of life, they gather and become a day, a year and a lifetime. That is the very life of the human.

To enumerate from below the ten worlds in our lives are: the world of hell, the world of hungry spirits, the world of animals, the world of asuras, the world of human beings, the world of heavenly beings, the world of voice-hearers, the world of cause-awakened ones, the world of Bodhisattvas, and the world of Buddhahood on the top. Just at the moment, Charles Lee was reading a book about "Ten World' Life" which shows a conversation between Dr. Toynbee and Ikeda. Here's a brief introduction to that.

Ikeda said.

"There is a view of life in the Buddhism called the 'Ten Worlds View'. This 'Ten Worlds View' divide the state of life into ten categories. And every living creature, including humans, is subject to show the life of 'ten worlds' at the moment by the conditions of that time. This way of thinking of the 'Ten Worlds', for example, is equivalent to hell, purgatory, and heaven, which Dante painted in 『Divina Commedia』. Dante's case was largely divided into the three worlds, but in the Buddhism, more precisely, the world is divided into the 'Ten Worlds'.

Ikeda explained the Ten Worlds easily from the world of hell to the world of Buddhahood. Dr. Toynbee wondered.

"In Buddhism, the psychology is analyzed with great sophistication and elaboration. That precision is superior to any psychological analysis ever studied in the West."

Ikeda also explained in detail, saying, "Ten suchnesses" written in the Chapter on Expedient Means of the Lotus Sutra is the laws of life, changing moment by moment. And asked the doctor's opinion about the law of causality in the Buddhism. The doctor said with enthusiasm.

"I think the law of life is karma. Actions must have consequences, and no one can escape from them. But the results are not irrevocable. The next action you do can change the results good or bad."

In the midst of Ikeda's explanation of "Ten suchnesses". Dr. Toynbee was really interested in that there was an alien exchange called 'Nidana' to form a 'cause' deep inside life. The doctor said in an excited voice.

"The idea of Ten suchnesses is not much different from what I think of as challenging and fighting back."

The idea of "challenging and fighting back" can be said to indicate what 'relationship' is of the party involved.

Ikeda also nodded and said.

"If the challenging and fighting back you are talking about is the phenomenon of the life itself, I think it's the same thing as cause and effect of life taught in the Buddhism. If there is a challenge, there will be fighting back. That's because there's a law of life."

The hearts of modern people are covered with thick dark clouds. The dark cloud clings so tightly that it is hard to fall off. Even if we want it to go away with shaking our hands, but it is always attached forever. If managed to chase away one dark cloud, another came in without any sound. The modern man's mind is not comfortable at all.

Thoughts are like clouds, they darken your mind when you have a lot of thoughts, and when you are confused, they also feel dizzy. An uneasy mind prevails because of the darkening of the mind and the foolishness of the mind. I hate anxiety, so I try to get rid of it, but rather, the clouds of thought are rising up, making my mind darker and dizzier.

But where on earth do those dark clouds come from?

Nietzsche said the reason is false idolatry and existing order, blaming them. But the view of Buddhism is a little different from Nietzsche.

In the Buddhism, people who live in a delusive world with ignorance and anguish are described as "Living Things(衆生)." In other words, the dark clouds held by modern people were originally in the human mind. It's nothing more than a revelation of a dark cloud inside the human mind.

This world is divided into light and darkness. Just like that, human life also develops and vanishes as light and darkness cross. In Buddhism terms, the light is called Buddhist doctrines(法性), and darkness is called ignorance(無明).

Life is, in some ways, a long journey that makes one's troubled dark life bright and shiny.

For whatever reason, if human unhappiness is caused by dark clouds in their hearts, it can be interpreted as a sign that driving out the dark clouds can make human happy.

So Nietzsche came down from the mountain to tell people how to be the superhuman, and how to drive out the dark clouds.

He says.

"I'm going to give and distribute. Until the wise among human rejoices their stupidity, and the poor rejoice their fullness.

To do that, I have to go down to that abyss. Like you, falling to the other side of the sea and reflect the summer every evening. You overflowing star!

I must fall as you. Like the people I'm going to meet down

there will say.

So bless me. You silent eyes! You who can see even great happiness without jealousy!

Bless this glass that is about to overflow! A glass out of which golden water flowing and to lighten up your joy to the whole world!"

Part 2

The last pattern of life

Nietzsche, the philosopher who bloomed modern philosophy. The philosopher of various nicknames.

The philosopher who achieved a turning point in intellectual history by shaking off the spirit of modernity, which can unite all things, politics, ideas, culture, and civilization that had been concentrated in modernity. The philosopher who has made the transition from modernity to contemporary.

A philosopher who overthrew Platonism which had been maintained throughout the 2,000-year history of Western philosophy. In other words, the philosopher of the hammer who destroys all the traditional Western identities of self-evidence. In addition, he is a philosopher who has various assessments.

People call the Nietzsche philosophy a mature 'Dionysian and positive philosophy'. Nietzsche said about everything existing in the world that "there is nothing to throw away, to be good without it" as a song of eternal positiveness to the life of a healthy human being.

Nietzsche's declaration of 'God is dead' may be said to mean not merely a religious dimension, but an end to European civilization penetrating Western intellectual history, and at the same time the Dharma of Nichiren, the great saint will bloom fancy, brilliant and artistic flower giving rise to the new culture.

When we recognize that the absolute value that man has sought so far is no longer worthy, we will be able to kill God, open a new horizon, fill water in the new sea, and the sun will rise again.

As we explore the truth, we will be able to be more honest about ourselves, and that honest mind makes our lives more clearly and can find our self-ego, which is our nature. This is a core concept of 'the death of God' called by Nietzsche.

Nietzsche says.

"If you have pursued heavenly values so far, now turn that gaze to yourself."

When the celestial value collapses, humans have no choice but to come down to earth and create new values to survive on this earth, but there are only two ways of living in this world. One is the way of life to be superhuman, and the other is the way of being the final or the last human. Nietzsche sometimes describes the last man as a 'Last species'

So what is the distinction between the two?

Do you still value love? Are you trying to create new values? What do you admire? Have you ever looked at the stars in the sky? Do you have a dream?

Nietzsche says.

Not only does a modern man have stars in his heart, and cannot conceive a new star. The human earth is still fertile enough to plant buds. But the land will one day be dry and lifeless. Then the trees will never grow from this land again.

It's sad! It won't be long before humans can no longer shoot the arrows of longing over their shoulders, and they can't buzz and make the bows ring!

As I tell you, to give birth to a dancing star, man must keep the chaos in himself.

It's sad! There will come a time when humans can't have stars anymore! It's sad! The age of despicable human beings, who can no longer despise themselves, is coming!

Behold! I will show you the human of the last species.

"What is love? What is creation? What is longing? What is the star?" The human of the last species asks blinking his/her eyes.

Then the earth becomes smaller, and on the earth, the human of the last species who dwarfs all things, leaping and jumping. This species is like a flea and cannot be eradicated. The human of the last species can live more than any others.

"We found happiness."

The human of the last species said blinking his/her eyes.

Every modern human understands himself as a human of his intrinsic character. Once you enter the crowd, your personality disappears and quickly turns into a gang of violent riots just like when the human of pride and greatness enters the crowd, it is hard to distinguish individuals.

The crowd is the existence of mystery. If you look at them one by one, they are clever and cunning enough to think they are good. And when they thought they might be in danger, they become a coward right away. However, when such individuals get together and become a group, their personalities change.

The changes are also varied. If you think it's a group of

gentle lambs, it quickly turns into a swarm of swarming pigs. In one time they shed tears at small happiness, and they make a fuss and even dies with drinking alcohol. But what good is it to despise or deplore the animal nature of the crowd? We have no choice but to face reality.

It wouldn't be too difficult to drive the crowd crazy about something. They always want to be crazy about something. It's because they want to fill empty lives with something. The crowd begins to run wild with the dangerous power on its back.

They, who have already turned violent, do not hesitate to act completely unpredictable. By moving according to only interests and pursuing only one's own benefits, he freely throws away his morals as a master that he followed well until now. As the human mind dries and dwarfs, the weight of life weighs heavily on its shoulders. The crowd, which has turned into a mob, is changed as nothing but a swarm of locusts covering the ground.

"Hanging on the horizon like a black cloud in the sky, it soon spread fan-shaped and covered the sky. Where they had come down even the leaves cannot be seen, and all turned into the wasteland suddenly."

It is about a swarm of locusts from one literary work that

instantly turns arable land into a desolate wasteland. The locusts rush into small food and scrape away everything without leaving anything.

Nietzsche expressed human of the last species in much harsher words than that. It was not a swarm of locusts but the swarm of poisonous flies.

"Where the solitude stops, the market starts. And where the market begins, there begins the uproar of great actors, and the swarms of poisonous flies begin to buzz."

That market is a place where people gather from various places. They gather for one's own benefit. People buy and sell things there. In the market, things like deceiving and cheating others are done naturally. This place is filled with them here.

In the past, we sought a way of living together with respecting common values, but now only individuals became important and they are doing anything to maximize their own interests rashly. This form of life is the life type of a swarm of poisonous flies, and this becomes the 'The last pattern of life'.

Nietzsche describes the scene like this.

"Run away, my friend, into your solitude. You are being stung by a swarm of poisonous flies. Run! To the place where the fierce wind blows!

About Nietzscheanism

Run into your solitude! You have lived too close to the dwarfs and the poor. Get out of sight of them! They are only watching for a chance to revenge you.

Your unspoken pride is always on their nerves. So watch out for the narrow-minded ones! They feel themselves dwarfed. So their meanness is burning towards you, sometimes faintly, sometimes strongly with an invisible vengeance.

Don't raise your hand to beat them up again! For they are multitudinous, and it is not your destiny to be a fly swatter.

These dwarfs and poor are immeasurable. Haven't you seen countless tall buildings crumbling because of raindrops and weeds?

You are not a stone. Nevertheless, you have already been hollowed out by many raindrops. And in the future, the drops of water will finally break and split you.

You are exhausted by a swarm of poisonous flies and have been stung by a hundred. You are now suffered deeply with hundreds of stings. You with the deep heart, you have too much pain even from small hurts. Before the hurt recovers, the same poisonous insect is crawling up on your hands."

The final style of life is described in Lotus Sutra 'The comparison of three wagons and the burning house' This is the summary of the story.

The wealth man of the family lived in a country. One day a fire broke out in the wealth man's house. At home, the children of the wealth man were playing, running around the room, without noticing the fire had broken out. the wealth man came up with a good idea after trying to figure out how to rescue the children. He said to the children, "Children! There are three fine wagons waiting outside that you wanted. Come out and have it!" He managed to get the children out. Then they gave the children the finest of the three large white wagons with cows(Lotus Sutra).

This tale is about the story of children(every living thing) playing in a world in the fire of anguish, being led by their father, the wealth man, climbing into the large white wagons, being led to a peaceful and happy path.

SGI President Ikeda says.

"We live in a time when human beings are difficult to live like a human. It's a so-called evil world and full of evil relationships. So to live like a human, you need a constant improving track. That is our practice asceticism of the teachings of Buddha. If the top stops, it will fall. It's because when it's stable, it is spinning at a furious rate.

Anyone is fine. Just stand beside. Be together listening, encouraging, and creating a spark of life like 'buzz' in their troubled hearts. The response of 'There are people who think about my work' opens up the living space of the afflicted wide.

If you have the feeling of 'Being with others', a human can always stand up. That's the power of life. That's why good relationships are so important. It's good knowledge taught in the Buddhism.

The way of saving me and others, and how to live right as a human, the Buddhism reveals the track. When we enter that track, we stabilize. Realizing own lives, we get to improve.

Humans have their own ideal way and beliefs. Everybody's trying desperately to get there. But isn't it human beings who are willing to treat others with mercy, but contrary to their heart, going to end up selfish lives? There are also setbacks and blockages in life. The key to success is whether or not you can overcome it with the strength of not losing anything. That's why we have to seek the Buddhism.

Encouraging humanism in the human mind, building the bridge of peace, the bridge of culture is the Buddhism. Faith is an infinite hope and unlimited vitality. In accordance with his own determination, any environment is becoming the fertile land.

The light distribution is discovering the treasure of wisdom and the power of the good in the land of human life to flower peace and happiness. And friendship brings humans together, connecting the world, and placing the golden bridge of peace.

The people are the sea. Many ships can travel when the sea is calm. Likewise, if people have strong friendships, trust and peace will be created. And that peaceful sea can be reached by ships of friendship at all dimensions. What we're going to do is creating 'a sea of humanity' and 'a sea of friendship' that connect the world."

Nietzsche told the meaning of the existence of the human as Ubermensch. If the human is to be the human, the meaning as the human can be obtained by the human, and to do it, they must be the Ubermensch. He told Ubermensch is the major term of the healthy human

Nietzsche says.

"Ubermensch is the honest human who lives natural life without ethical pretense, enlightened, accepting the world as reality above the metaphysical illusion."

Around the 19th century, the big change was in the world.

Nietzsche read that periodical change correctly and led the change in a decisive manner. He ended the modernity and opened up the contemporary.

Nietzsche is the philosopher who wants to kill the god and save the human. Many people feel bad emotions about killing the god, but Nietzsche doesn't pay attention to it, instead, he pays attention to the human

Nietzsche says.

"Love your fate. Overcome the destiny on and on. You shall bear the tragedy. Life without suffering doesn't exist. Everyone has pain and agony. Regarding loving life, what shall we love. To love the pain is the practice of changing the value of the pain, and feeling the wind not as wind, not as reverse wind, but as the sweet wind that makes me fly. This is the life."

Nietzsche says again.

"Nobodies are on your side. Only the ocean and the desert located around you. You are within an endless void. You are the existence that should spread your wings now. You are the existence that should know the wisdom of using the wind. Nobody will help you. So love your destiny. Overcome the destiny on and on."

Part 3

The rope hanging over an abyss

When Zarathustra enters the closest city from the forest, he saw crows gathered around the market. Soon there will be the tightrope walking by the clown. Zarathustra told to the crowd like this.

"All of you, I want to teach you the superhuman. Human is a thing that needs overcoming. What did you do to overcome yourself?

Until now, every existence created something above itself. However, does all of you want to return to the animal rather than to overcome oneself and to be the tide in the middle of the ebb?

Look, I teach you the superhuman!

Superhuman is the will of the land. Let your own

volition to tell. The superhuman should be the will of the land!

Brothers, I tell you sincerely, and you should be loyal to the land. And don't believe people who talk about the hope about heaven! They are people who put poison and spread it if they knew it or not.

Zarathustra ended his word and thought in mind looking the crowd in silence. They are just laughing and standing up. They do not understand my word, and my mouth is not suitable to their ears."

And he added like this.

"Human is the rope between the animal and the superhuman(Ubermensch). The rope hanging over an abyss. Crossing to the other side, being in the middle of the rope, looking back, trembling and holding position are all dangerous.

The greatness of the human and why they can be lovable is that he/she is the being of passing by and falling.

I love. Who loves the virtue of oneself. The virtue is the very will of fall and the arrow of longing. This guy is crossing the bridge using their mind"

It is the writing of the preface of 「Thus Spoke Zarathustra」, which is the Nietzsche's major work.

'The rope hanging over an abyss', What other words can be, explicitly expressed like this? Yes, The life is distinctly the rope hanging over an abyss as Nietzsche told.

Nietzsche wants to say that life never allows the carelessness of one inch. Nevertheless, life is not the continuation of the tension like the rope hanging over an abyss. In the human lives, endless many beauty flows, brilliantness like the morning glow is shining, and the breathing of the peace blows. Meanwhile, the romance flows, love breaths, and friendship start.

Can't we live relaxed with putting that warm and rich mind in the base of the life? Cannot human live like that? To make the world like that, to make that utopia, Nietzsche continues his struggle.

What does it mean to be born as a human? It is a chance to open up a new life. The precious chance to lead one's live by oneself. The chance to transfer to the track of happiness. We were not born to be locked with an invisible chain and only to be dragged while crying. Nietzsche wanted to say like that.

In the 'The rope hanging over an abyss', the keyword is the word 'fall'. The word 'fall' Nietzsche tell is the meaning of reforming as the more honorable and valuable life, which is to be the master of one's life calling 'the will of the power', Ubermensch, throwing out the lives which cannot be said as happiness, which should be thrown away if it can be thrown away.

We are all people of riding on the tightrope. If we go to this side we live like animals, and to that side, we live like Ubermensch. We are the existence of moving between them. Which part to choose is up to oneself.

Why should we be the Ubermensch?

It is because it makes us human. It is the token of the human for us. It gives the meaning to human existence. If we are not the Ubermensch, we are not human anymore. We just live like being like animals.

We also can be an artist of life. Not ending in my happiness, we are to be the master of life changing the world. Finally, we are to be the master of the world.

Nietzsche says.

Where is not the abyss that human stands? Looking doesn't mean that looking inside the abyss? Courage is the best murderer. Courage kills vertigo in front of the abyss. Courage kills even death. It is because the courage can say that "Was it the truly human life? Okay! Then, once again".

Human is the bravest animal. Therefore human overcame every animal. Human overcame pain playing the music of the victory. Even if the human's pain was the much deepest pain...

SGI President Ikeda says.

"The fighting person with braveness has the lively motion of life. The whistle of hope resonates. The pulsation of the delight flows strongly. And the absolute respect and affection of happiness will be open surely.

Generally human is the great existence, and what's inside the mind can change a life. Because the human mind is like the water, and like the shape of water changes according to the container, the life changes.

The story seems like the jump of logic, it is just like a cup of water inside the glass. If the water inside the cup is pure, and the diamond in it can be seen, however, if the water inside the cup is muddy and dirty that treasure cannot be seen. The best treasure inside human life, the diamond is Buddha nature, Ubermensch

However human cannot get rid of the dirty water inside one's life. It falsely sounds like eliminating oneself. Inside oneself, there is me(我). Ego(自我) means the glass nothing else, and the glass which is the true nature of oneself never changes. It is eternal like the life of the universe. It just exists in repeating life and death. Even if I consider the life of the universe, the only difference is the body and soul, the life itself is unchanging

If we call the sea as the great universe, the wave from appearing to disappearing and from disappearing to appearing is our life. The wave and the sea cannot be separate. The wave is one action of the sea.

Early Goethe told in 「Faust」 "Everything makes up the whole. Each one is moving and living with each other.". The whole means the universe life and each moving and living one means our life.

The dirty water inside the cup is the dark figure of tangled evil deeds(惡行) made by itself through the numerous three works(三業) of the body(身), mouth(口), and intention(意), and it leads us to the unhappiness. People with many good deeds can live a happy life somehow, however, the number of that people didn't seem to be many.

What is the greatness of a human. What is nobility. The contem porary society is only for the social position and economic power, the norm cannot be seen.

If we cannot recognize the goal of life, even the one succeed in life extremely, the real sense of fulfillment and happiness cannot be felt.

The great universe is inside the human mind which is the very object of the three thousand realms in a single moment of life(一念三千). The human has good, evil and unlimited possibility with a lively motion in a moment.

When young or at the one period of life human can use desperate power, however, to maintain and accomplish that power is really hard to find. That way the finalization of oneself cannot happen and the contribution to human happiness and the realization of the peace. Every effort until then come to nothing.

Pure and fresh air goes way by time flies and falls into a habitual routine. In this way, the new development never happens. To break the habitual routine, we need to go back to the starting point."

Zarathustra's first speech was over. The yelling and cheering of the crowd stopped his speech. The crowd yelled.

"Ah, Zarathustra, Give the human of the last species to us. Make us to the human of the last species! And we will give you the superhuman!"

The crowd smiles while saying this.

"Dear Zarathustra, you shall rather be superhuman! We found the happiness and are happy with it."

Meanwhile, every crowd was yelling and smacked their lips. However, the sad Zarathustra thought in his mind.

'They cannot understand me. I'm not a suitable mouth to their ears. Maybe I listened to only the shallow stream and trees for a too long time living in the forest.

My soul is without wobble and bright like the morning mountain. However, they think I'm the cold guy, sneer who is talking horrible jokes.

Now they are laughing watching us. They even hated me laughing. There is ice inside their smile.

In no time the evening has come and the market is going in the darkness. The crowd scattered. Usually, curiosity and terror languish.

At that moment, one guy came to the Zarathustra and whispered to his ear.

"Zarathustra, leave this city. Many people here hate you. Even good and right people hate you, saying you as an enemy and contemnor. Even believers of the right faith hate you and saying that you are a dangerous person. It was lucky they just laughed at you at that extent. You saved your life because you lowered yourself. So soon leave this city."

Finally, the night has come and the cold wind grazed Zarathustra's side. He stood up and eventually left the market.

In this part, the Nietzsche's 'The rope hanging over an abyss' story ends. And Nietzsche didn't tell us the scene of crossing on the tightrope over the abyss. He just simply wrote, "The virtue is the very will of fall and the arrow of longing. This guy is crossing the bridge using their mind"

Dear readers, do you remember?

Do you remember 'the way of practicing asceticism' the Nietzsche wanted to finalizes with everything he had?

He wanted to notify in passion 'the way of practicing asceticism' for anyone to be superhuman. It is because he wanted to find out people who have the same will. With them, he wanted to advance to the road of becoming superhuman. However, at the last moment, he had no choice but to give up his great dream. Nietzsche could never notify 'the way of practicing asceticism'. What was the problem?

『Thus Spoke Zarathustra』 is both nominally and virtually Nietzsche's major work. And this work's climax can be called as nothing but 'The rope hanging over an abyss'. This is because to be a superhuman we need to cross to the Ubermensch's side on the rope.

Nietzsche's philosophy consists of 'God's death', 'will to power', 'eternal recurrence' and 'inversion of truth', but the climax is always going to the point of Ubermensch of 'the life's master should be human!' Nietzsche spread his philosophy and idea to this one point.

Nietzsche wanted to let us know the secret of being super human he realized. However, sadly he never showed the scene of crossing on 'The rope hanging over an abyss' to the Ubermensch's side. Actually, it was impossible to show it.

Instead of Nietzsche, Charles Lee will sum up the end part of the 'The rope hanging over an abyss'

Finally, people with courage came one by one. They encouraged each other and climbed up the hill. It was to be on the rope hanging over an abyss.

Their faces ware bright as morning glow and their mind was

Nietzsche and Ikeda

burning with the sense of duty to represent human. Because human is a peculiar existence when devoting oneself the power will be given.

They nodded looking at each other. Already there was no fear at all. Only the strongness of the guy between life and death. They were armed with risking one's life of crossing that rope without fail.

When they were close, it was known that everyone was wearing thing necklace on their neck alike. The silver necklaces. On the center of the hanging necklace was something and it was hard to see covered by clothes. In my opinion, it may be the token of the belief. Maybe because of it, all of them acted like believers. They actually tried to cross over an abyss by the power of belief

Finally, they came up to 'The rope hanging over an abyss', Then, something strange happened. By time flies, their confidence became big, and that confidence changed into the belief and the rope changed into a thicker rope.

Shortly, the thicker rope changed into the narrow path leading them to the mountain. The braves advanced wiping golden sweat flowing down. To the apex of the mountain, they advanced whistling with a pleasant mind.

About Nietzscheanism

Part 4

___

Who is the superman?

Zarathustra directly went to the market descending the mountain. He went there because there were a lot of people were there. He taught the existence of superhuman to the crowd. However, the crowd didn't understand what he talks. It is impossible to know if the crowds cannot understand his word or just ignored even they knew the meaning

Anyhow, Zarathustra was nothing but a laughing stock. However, we need to pay attention to the place of his first speech was the market. He wanted everyone to be superhuman. He thaught common people can be superhuman.

However, without spreading his will, he left the market

without warm hospitality from crowds gathered in the market, inevitably.

Zarathustra came back to the mountain that he lived. He was in the cave's solitude avoiding people And lived like the farmer who waits for harvest after sowing. However, his soul was in haste, and the longing to the people he loved became ardent.

It is because he had so much to give. In other words, cupping the hand once open with a loving mind, and being the giver with the shame was a really hard thing.

Zarathustra slept for a long time. Not only morning glow but also the sunshine of the morning passed on his head. Finally, his eyes opened. Zarathustra saw the forest, silence and inner side of himself with surprised eyes. Then suddenly yelled like the sailor who found out the land. He realized a new truth. Therefore he told like this.

One ray of the light came up. I need a traveling companion. A companion with whom I will go to the place where I want to go.

I was looking for the person, Zarathustra. The person creating, harvesting and making festivals with him. I'm with the creator, harvester, and festival maker. I'll show them rainbow, the stairs to superhuman.

Early, sacred soul looked the body in greed with an eye of the contempt. Until that time that was the best despising. Noble soul waited the dirty body gets thinner, ugly and hungry. Wasn't it sacred soul's way of entering to the heaven's door fleeing from the land of our body.

However, ah! the very soul itself become thin, ugly and hungry. Cruelty, this was the soul's pleasure.

"Brothers, tell me. The thing that your body tells about your soul? Your soul itself is just the complacency of poverty, dirt, and painfulness?

Yes. Human is dirty river water. So we need to be the sea first. Not to be dirty and accept dirty river water.

Look, I teach you superhuman. Superhuman is the sea, and your big contempt can sink inside it."

Zarathustra descended the mountain and looked up a traveling companion again. His goal was to meet the large group of people between the human of the last species and the superhuman. His itinerary was not to charging into one road. He passed thousands of paths and thousands of hidden islands of life.

Meeting with 'human of above dimension' was among

Nietzsche and Ikeda

it. His heart was full of hope anyone can be superhuman, and the belief again became the fire of sympathy.

Zarathustra said.

There are so many morning-glows not yet shine. where can we find the new morning and the mild red light opening the new morning which didn't discover before?

Nietzsche is the writer who often uses metaphors.

"Yes. Human is dirty river water. So we need to be the sea first. Not to be dirty and accept dirty river water.

Look, I teach you superhuman. Superhuman is the sea, and your big contempt can sink inside it."

Nietzsche compares the human from river water and superhuman from the sea. The metaphor of him comparing human from the river water is a right and great expression. It is because the river flows to the sea with everything thick and dirty.

However, even Nietzsche compares superhuman to the sea, he didn't tell the reason for comparing superhuman to the sea.

In this point, I want to notice the thoughts of Charles Lee about superhuman and the sea Nietzsche told.

Firstly, I'd like to say about superhuman. Superhuman doesn't mean the special person, but the general person. The general person like us who live in the will of the land following the rule of nature.

Superhuman, Nietzsche saying, Ubermensch have 2 meanings in my estimation. Firstly, the process of trying to be superhuman through the Ubermensch styled life. In other words, the braves enter the road to be superhuman. and secondly, only after the process of 'practicing asceticism' the luster of life can be gotten, that is the person who shows the light of the personality.

Then what does the sea mean?

Sea is nature and the universe life itself. In other words, it is the nature of the Buddha. The nature of the Buddha is the 'Universe life's power' which supports every living thing with unlimited life power and unlimited wisdom and mercy. To add more, the sea is the existence of richness and fulfillment being filled with everything.

By the way, the winding river water flows into the sea with dirty water. Human also finalizes once deficient and unfinished oneself with various experiences in life. Isn't it that kind of meaning for Nietzsche to compare the river water to human and the sea to superhuman?

In Lotus Sutra, it is explained like this.

"Inside the sea, there are numerous treasures, but the river water is not like it. The sea is getting deep, but the river water is not like it. The sea vast and boundless, but the river water is not like it. The sea makes body visit, but the river water is not like it. The sea doesn't increase or decrease even it accepts big rain and river water, but the river water is not like it. The sea has the fluctuation of the tide, but the river water is not like it. The sea's salinity is stable, but the river water is not like it.

The sea has 9 kinds of virtues, but the river water has much loss."

In my opinion, Nietzsche knew much more knowledge than generally known.

SGI President Ikeda says.

"In the Latter Day of the Law with confusing society and religion, to save human and change the period, opening up and teaching the nature of the Buddha which everyone has. In other words, to save people of the Latter Day of the Law, there is no way but to develop the great possibility inside the human.

Lotus Sutra is teaching 'humanism'. Because it can only

be started from the human, and having been found a great possibility in human life, it is called 'humanism'.

The humanism in the Buddhism is not based on the rationality or the shape similar to the god. The humanism in the Buddhism is based on the possibility of the human revolution through the development of Buddha nature.

Every life is the very form of an excellent method. So, life itself is equal. Therefore every life in open to the excellent method and has Buddha nature. Among them, the human can represent in everyday life through Buddhist commandments' power. That's why the 'mind' is important.

The humanism taught in the Buddhism's premise is always to practice it to revolutionize one's life by oneself.

The Latter Day of the Law are 'the period of the fight' in one word. Everything flows into the direction of fighting. The power compelling to it is the strong conviction of 'Believing Buddha nature of me and others!'. And the practice of that conviction is nothing more than 'actions of respecting people'.

The Buddhism is 'the action(行)'. The action is practicing the thing he/she resolved even with any difficulties. If there is no effort to overcome by oneself's power, it cannot be called 'the action'. Trying to accomplish that resolution to the end, and there is no other way but to enter the Nirvana, that is to be superhuman."

It can be said that the story Nietzsche wanted to tell us was about the Ubermensch, superhuman. And the superhuman in his mind was generally person like us, not the special human being. How that general person can be superhuman? It is conservative to say that it has all of Nietzscheanism.

One professor who is in research of Nietzscheanism told like this.

"Under the change of paradigm of collapse existing value system and the system of existence, people cannot avoid panic and anxiety. Regarding this, didn't Nietzsche wanted to tell to them the message of 'Not only bad world that remains to us. This is the real world and we can make it lovable and positive if we want. Superhumans are people who work for mankind's future together.'?

Nietzsche clearly said.

"If the philosophy doesn't connect to the practice in life, what is its value will be based?"

Like his word, even if Nietzsche's will is great, if that cannot be proved by the real figure, the power of the Nietzscheanism will be finally halved.

So Nietzsche started writing 「will to power」 after finishing the writing of 「Thus Spoke Zarathustra」. He wanted to show 'the way of practicing asceticism' clearly. He went nap on finalizing this project. To accomplish this he ignited himself as much as he wanted.

However, even after the 3 years and a few months of his sorrowful struggle, he couldn't show the way of practicing asceticism to us. By then, he looked up the sky and kneeled lamenting his limit of ability. This is the very moment when he lost mustache and hair. What was the problem? That story is going to be explained in Part 7, 'The last battle'.

By the way, as I mentioned before, the people who flowered Nietzsche's philosophy were Buddhist believer's organization, SGI members. And they entered into being superhuman not through Nietzscheanism, but through Lotus Sutra. Within the profound Buddhist writings, there was 'the way of practicing asceticism' that Nietzsche was looking for.

That story will be explained in Part 8, 'A picture of Mandara'

Part 5

---

3 kinds of tales of transformation

Thus Spoke Zarathustra.

"Listen up. I'm going to say to you three changes of mind. For the mind how to be a camel, for the camel how to be a lion and for the lion how to be a child. What are differences of camel, lion, and child's mind?

The first animal is the camel.

Look at this animal precisely. This is the animal with strong endurance as you know. Just the heat of the desert cannot make it fall. Even without Oasis for several days, it is fine.

Also, it's back is so wide and solid that it easily carries the heavy load. The thing you should pay attention to is the knee of the camel. Look at the callus of knee well. It is really respectful. You can't imagine how many times it kneels. So polite and good animal it is.

However, I imagine how many hurts this animal gave to its mind. It made the master's pride honorable by kneeling down often, but at the same time, it strongly hurt its pride.

No matter how dirty the water is, he is willing to go in without nagging, even if there are all kinds of ugly frogs or toads living there. It's a quiet walk with all the load on it. I've never heard this animal say "No" to its owner.

I think about the life of this animal. I think about how this good animal is torturing his life. Did his sacrifice really come from his good heart? Or is it himself that made his life so hard that he had to call it a sacrifice?

Don't you think life is hard, making it a pain that you have to endure? If so, you have made your world a desert. Didn't tell you. The Spirit of Gravity wants you to be so good.

We are all camels. The camel is very patient and carries no matter how heavy its load is, but what we should note is his knee bone.

Though he always kneels down with pride for his

master, so he is patient and endurable and carries a heavy load, but the thing we should pay particular attention to is not the endurance of it, but the habit of slavery that talks about the endurance. So when the camel meets the world, it becomes a desert.

About the second story, the lion.

I've never seen an animal like this that won't listen to others. He who wants to order something to this animal have to risk his own life. When you try to do something, it will growl.

This animal has a desire for freedom. If a camel had succeeded in the transformation to become a lion, he would no longer serve any master. He will make the desert his kingdom.

One day I saw a lion fighting a dragon with golden scales. Perhaps the lion was on his way to confront the last master, God, over all the masters he had defeated. The lion did not know, but in fact, the dragon was a disguised God

Because the spirit of the lion was not willing to admit God, God had no choice but to appear as a dragon. The dragon said.

"You must do this."

What do you think the dragon's words mean?

You've heard a lot of dragon's word. The dragon speaks to the lion. You must obey this rule. You have to do this way. The voice of a dragon is the voice of morality, the voice of law, and the voice of custom or institution.

The dragon said again. The value of all things shines from me. He said he was not only a creator of values but a man who valued them. Then the lion growled and shouted:

"I want to do this."

He listens to no one's orders, only to follow his own desires. Leave me alone. I don't want to follow orders from anyone. I want freedom.

The dragon disputes. All values are already created, and I'm the all values created.

I want you to see this beast again. Why should the mind not to stay on the camel? Why does the mind need a lion? Is there anyone here who dreams of winning freedom, creating values? Then you must be a lion first.

Brothers, to be free and to be able to say the sacred 'no'

Nietzsche and Ikeda

to duties you must first be a lion.

If a camel becomes a lion, it is a huge profit. In the eyes of the camel, the lion's actions will be seen as plunder. However, a camel, who loved to be ordered, must find an illusion and arbitrariness in order to come to freedom.

There must be threats or compulsion and coercion. Sometimes there will be great temptations. If you're sunbathing in the yellow sand, how can't you look sideways when there are so many springs?

But a lion succumbed to thirst and did not become like a comfortable camel. He knows that wherever there is an oasis there is also idol worship.

Do you remember when I wrote 'humane too humane'? Remember that I had the courage of even burning my returning boat? Being lonely and hungry rather than comfortable with God, at that moment my spirit was surely a lion.

God constantly commands us. This must be done, this must be done like this. It is the voice of morality, the voice of law, the voice of God and the voice of the world.

What is important here is for the lion to growl and reveal the will of its desire, "I want to do it." This is really important. It's the nobility of the mind.

So when a camel meets the world, it becomes a desert, but when a lion meets the world, it becomes a kingdom. Where there is an oasis, there must also be idol worship. That idolatry, that is God's institution, God's law, God's world, morality, and sociology. It is the nobility of the mind that can reveal one's own desire to say no to the idolatry.

But the lion was tired of fighting the dragon.

So far I have told you about the spirit by which camels become lions. Aren't you curious about the fate of a lion fighting against a dragon? The lion fought fiercely with the dragon. Unfortunately, however, the lion could not completely defeat the dragon.

Although it did not admit the dragon's dominance, it is concerned about how long it will be able to endure the ongoing battle.

A lion did not make life a desert like a camel, but its life was not something to laugh and enjoy. It was like a soldier driven into an unknown war. What was the problem? It rebelled against the dragon saying no, but then it could not say what itself could do.

It knew only what it hated, but it didn't know much about what it liked. Even if it had taken freedom from the dragon, it did not know how to use it.

About the third story, a child.

You look at the children over there. Those children's minds are in the third stage. The mind should be a child. I don't know if you'll ask me. How can a child do something that even a lion could not do? Why should a lion who used to rob freedom be a child now? I'll answer this.

A child is an innocent man, oblivion, a new beginning, a play, a self-rolling wheel, the first exercise, and sacred affirmation. A child is faithful to his own desires. Morality, law, or system cannot be applied to a child. This is because a child has no stings of conscience. A child can only laugh innocently.

Do you know the difference from a lion? The child doesn't growl. He/she just smiles. The child laughs at the dragon. The dragon, who was the competitor of the lion, is not the competitor of the child. If the dragon had appeared, it would have become a child's toy.

The third transformation is, after all, a child. A child

can be superhuman. This is because children are endless positiveness and the new creation that can constantly transform oneself.

Man must move from slave morality to master morality, as a child, to creative morality.

Charles Lee says,

Nietzsche tells the story of the transformation of the camel into a lion and the spirit of a lion into a child again. Through this story, he tries to show us how ordinary people become superhuman. But in the end, what humans experience in the real world is just a 'the style of camel's life.' The rest end up in fiction.

Well, three changes are actually possible. But that is only in special cases that can be represented through the world of faith. The fantastic story of the camel becoming a lion and the spirit of the lion being a child certainly exists in the world of faith.

Faith may seem weak at first glance, but it can be said that it is actually the strongest thing in the world. This is because the power of faith can be used to create existence(有) from nothing(無).

In the world of faith, mysterious things such as '3 kinds

of tales of transformation' often happen. Faith is invisible. However, the change in life, which is becoming unknown through the life of faith, appears as 'a mature character' in reality. The power of faith is not directed toward God, but by the painstaking 'human revolution' that he tried to transform himself.

Buddhism explains this '3 kinds of tales of transformation' in a slightly different angle from Nietzsche. How is it explained? Now, I'm going to introduce you to a passage from the writings of the great saint Nichiren, the scriptures of the Latter Day of the Law.

"Lotus Sutra is not that complex. Talking and guessing the past and future's thing correctly. To know the reason of the past, look at the result of the present. And to know the future's result, look at which reason do you making now."

As the passage said above, "In Buddhism, human life is perpetuated by the repetition of life and death from the past." The present life is also connected to the past and finally made this way. In that life, everything he has done in the past has melted in and created karma to live as a present life.

I think it is a great metaphor to compare human life to a camel. Human beings, knowing or not, live in chains of invisible karma. The question only depends on whether the task is bright and blessed karma that leads to a happy life, or dark karma filled with misery. So Nietzsche exclaims, "Dear you, cut off the chains binding you and live as masters of life!"

Many people point to their lives and say, "I feel injustice." It may sound natural for them to say so. He does his best, but as always, nothing improves. He is like a soldier who is driven into an unknown war. What was the problem?

Man does not know that there is a past in his life now. I wouldn't pay much attention to the fact even if I knew it. As long as you're born as a human being, you'll see the world you want to live in one day, and then you'll be able to say with confidence, "I finally became a happy person too."

But the message that Buddhism throws at us is as determined and clear as cutting a radish with a knife. "Do you really want to be happy? Then, change your dark karma first!"

Let me introduce you to another page of the writings of Nichiren.

"Leaving the house of original enlightenment, nothing will be a delight. I only want following the wonderful low of 'safe and stable present life' and 'good deed of future life', and it becomes the good memories of the present life. I say to you that gather mind as one call it Nam-myoho-renge-ko(Lotus Sutra), and encouraging it to others will only be the good memory of present life."

"House of original enlightenment" has no other meaning. It's about finding yourself. Who am I? Where did I come from and where am I going? Ask yourself and set off.

Then, I'd like to present you with an episode about "House of original enlightenment".

This happened when SGI President Ikeda was still a young man. It is the first time a young Ikeda meets his future mentor, Josei Toda.

Summer of 1947, Japan, Tokyo.

There was some silence. But the intimate atmosphere there was still hovering around in warmth. It was then.

"Sir!"

Suddenly, Ikeda's strong voice broke the silence. All

eyes were focused on him.

"There's something I want to be taught, but...."

Toda stared at Ikeda with his eyes squinted over his glasses.

"What is it? I'll listen to anything."

"Sir! What does the right life mean? The more I think about it, the more I cannot find the answer"

"Ah, this is a very difficult question."

Toda put out his cigarette and said smiling,

"I don't think there is a single person who can answer this question correctly today. However, I can answer it. Because of good luck, I managed to read the Buddhism of the great saint, Nichiren, the philosophy of life, with my body a little."

Toda's quiet words were brimming with confidence.

"There are many difficult problems in our long lives. The current food shortage, the housing shortage are examples. Also, life, economics, or love affairs, disease, war, family issues are like that. It's the life that you don't know what's going to happen. Every time, people suffer from bone-cutting pain. But this kind of distress is something like the sleep of a wave that's relatively easy.

There is a fundamental pain in life that cannot be solved. The question of how to solve the problem of life and death in order to be the right human being is that. There is no such thing as a true and proper life unless the right solution is made to birth, old age, sickness, and death in Buddhism. I can't do something to already born myself even if I say that it was wrong to be born.

Toda's funny way of saying things almost burst everyone into laughter. But the story was so important that people waited for his next story, holding back their laughter.

"Even if someone thinks she wants to be a 19-year-old virgin and never wants to get old, she will be a grumpy old lady after 40 to 50 years. Even if I say I hate diseases, I cannot avoid getting diseases. This can't be avoided, either. And the death at the end of the day is so strict. Everyone thinks they can live forever, but everyone here will be dead in 60 to 70 years. It's no use saying you don't want to die. No matter how high you are, no matter how rich you are.

This fundamental problem in life is a sad fact that you can't help saying that you have a strong belief. It would be fair to say that there has never been a philosophy that has solved this critical problem in life in a more correct and wonderful way. So even if you wanted to have the right life, nobody couldn't do anything.

Even if you dig into the deep fundamental problems of life, you will fail to know them, so there's a fool who commit suicide because life is hard to know. You have no choice but to be pessimistic, to be in the present, or to be foolish and spend your life being resigned.

But the great saint Nichiren is now solving this difficult problem of life, the essence of life. Furthermore, he specifically teaches any man and wife to become such life respect and affection. Where on earth exist great philosophy of life like this?"

Ikeda had a hunch. The meeting appears to be a religious sect of the great saint Nichiren, but he is not a monk. It is so different from those unenlightened elders who were drumming in common white clothes that he used to see when he was young.

Toda went on talking pulling a cigarette.

"It's good to think about what is the right life. But in the time of thinking, take action of the philosophy of life of the great saint Nichiren. Aren't you still young? Someday you'll find out that you're walking the right life even if you don't like to know. I can say it's as clear as this."

Toda lit a cigarette saying so.

At the moment Ikeda's eyes shone.

"I'd like to ask you one more thing. What kind of man does a true patriot mean?"

Toda spoke easily, enjoying his cigarette.

"It's simple. Kusunogi Masashi is also a patriot. Yoshida Shogindo is also a patriot. Captain Nogi is also a patriot. Certainly. But as you can see from this, the concept of patriots changes with the times. A person who is loyal to a nation or ethnic group is a patriot, but that country and the ethnic group itself change very much along with the changing of the period. Therefore, the human character of patriots also changes.

If there is a timeless true patriot, it can be concluded that he is a believer of the wonderful law. The reason for this is that a believer of the wonderful law is to save a noble human being forever and to be the base of building a truly happy society that will not fall apart from the

About Nietzscheanism

current unhappy nation. It is so natural that a person who believes the wonderful law and practices it will have the best patriot's qualification. This is not idealism at all. A national society based on the wonderful law will emerge in no doubt.

Until then, many people may not believe it. But when you see them, you will be surprised. There is certainly such power in the Buddhism of the great saint, Nichiren, Nam-myoho-renge-ko. I think a historian will certainly acknowledge this point in 100 to 200 later."

Toda finished the story like reaching the distant future. There was a clear answer in the insignificant talk. You may want to talk more deeply through teaching. However, it seemed to have ended with a rough argument because it was impossible for the young Ikeda to understand it any more.

After the fateful meeting, the young Ikeda took Toda Josei as his mentor and walked the path of 'mentor and disciple'.

In Buddhism, path of 'mentor and disciple' becoming a Buddha is called the 'The Golden Road'

Part 6

———

The woman and the man

Going down the street alone at sunset, Zarathustra met an old woman. The old woman told him this.

"Zarathustra, you've told our women many things just like men. But you've never said anything about a woman."

Then he said to the old woman.

"When it comes to women, it would be better to tell the men."

Then the old woman said,

"Tell me about a woman, too. I'm so old that I'll soon forget whatever I hear."

So he decided to accept the old woman's request and said:

"For a woman, everything is a riddle.

A man is a tool for a woman. The purpose is always in the child. So, what is a woman to a man?

A true man wants two things: danger and play. Therefore, men want women as dangerous toys.

Men should be educated for combat and women should be educated for the relaxation of men who are warriors. Everything else is foolish.

Warriors don't like too sweet fruit. That's why warriors like women. This is because even the sweetest woman tastes bitter.

A child is hidden inside a real man. This child wants to play. So, now, you women, find the child hidden in the man!

May a ray of starlight shine in your love! I wish your hope is, "I want to give birth to a superhuman!".

May there be courage in your love Let you strike with love to the terror-striking man.

Men, when a woman makes love, be afraid of it. For a woman in love sacrifices, everything and everything else becomes worthless to her.

Men, when a woman hates you, be afraid. For a man's soul is only evil at the bottom, but a woman's soul is

Nietzsche and Ikeda

mean at the bottom.

Who does the woman hate the most? The iron rod said to the magnet:

"I hate you no more than you pull me in. It's because I'm not strong enough to hold"

A man's happiness lies in 'I want.' But a woman's happiness lies in 'He wants.'

Therefore, a woman must discover the depth of her surface through obedience. The surface is a woman's heart, a skin that fluctuates violently over shallow water.

But the man's heart is deep and it flows with the sound of 'Splash' through the cave beneath the ground. A woman may faintly feel the power of a man, but she cannot understand it.

Slaves and tyrants were hidden in women's hearts for too long. Therefore, women still cannot form friendships. Women only know love. But say it. You men! Which of you has the ability to make friendships?

Ah, you men, how poor and stingy your soul is!"

Then the old woman answered him.

"You Zarathustra just said many interesting things. Especially for young women who are fitted with your word.

It's strange. Zarathustra knows very little about a woman, but somehow he's strikingly right about a woman!

Now, get a little truth as a token of your gratitude! I'm old enough to know this truth!

Cover this with a cloth and cover the mouth. If you don't, it will make a big noise. It means this little truth."

"Give me your little truth, old woman!" he said. Then the old woman answered.

"You're going to the girls? Then don't forget this whip!"

This is what Zarathustra said.

Here, I'd like to ask readers for your understanding. Lotus Sutra used by Charles Lee is not the original writing of Lotus Sutra, but rather the writing of the great saint Nichiren. The writing of the Nichiren means a collection of letters toward his disciples explaining Lotus Sutra intelligibly.

The great saint Nichiren had several disciples. Among them were monks and members of the married family. There were many women believers among the members of the married family. For some reason, his writing contains many stories about men and women. Especially, there are many articles about a woman's nature.

The following phrases are written about a woman's mind. It will be of great help to a man who wants to understand a woman's mind, which is both foggy and mysterious. I summarized a few of them.

"A woman is like a vine, and a man is like a pine tree, if they are apart even in one moment, they cannot stand up."

"A woman is a body that is following things and makes you follow things."

"It is the power of the bow that makes the arrow fly, and the power of the dragon that the cloud flows to, and the deeds of the husband is the power of the wife."

"A man will give up his life because of shame, and a woman will give up her life for a man."

"The water is soft, so it flows in and out of the way. A woman, in the same way, when confronted by a man's strong heart, is blocked and directed in the wrong direction."

"If a woman's husband is a thief, she will be a thief.

About Nietzscheanism

If the husband is in delight, his wife is prosperous. It is like shadows and bodies, flowers and berries, roots and leaves."

"A woman is a mother. All of us should think of becoming Buddha because of the grace of endless reincarnation."

"A woman takes her husband a soul, and without a husband, there is no woman's soul."

"As a woman's body, you have placed yourself to Lotus Sutra in this dirty world, even Brahma the Creator will see with his noble eyes."

"For a woman, Lotus Sutra is to be the lamp in the dark, a ship in the sea, and a guardian in the fear."

"Lotus Sutra is superior to all the other sutra and it is as the king of land runners, Lion King, and the king of flying creatures, Eagle. It is impossible for a woman who believes in Lotus Sutra to be led by the sins of the world to fall into evil ways."

Lotus Sutra says that women can also become Buddha. In all the Buddhist scriptures before Lotus Sutra, saying "Women is a roasted seed which could have been Buddha," rejected woman being Buddha. However, in Lotus Sutra, 'Entering Nirvana of the women' is happening.

So here's some good news for the female reader. It's news about 'Entering Nirvana of the women'.

Here, I would like to introduce you a letter sent by the great saint Nichiren to his female disciple.

> I've received a lot of Things. There is no moon in the thick waters, no birds in the dry trees, and no Buddha in the body of a woman without a mind(心). A woman with Lotus Sutra is like clear water, so there will be a moon of Buddha. To compare it, a woman doesn't know herself well at the beginning of her pregnancy, but when the months go by and the days go by, she sure of pregnancy.
>
> You can tell whether a sensible woman is a boy or a girl, and Lotus Sutra is the same. If you believe in Nam-myoho-renge-ko(南無妙法蓮華經), you will have your heart at home and the women will be pregnant with Buddha. I don't know well at first, but as the months go by, the Buddha of the mind will appear in dreams and gradually come out with joy.
>
> There are a lot of Buddhism, but I'll quit. Following

Lotus Sutra seems easy, but it is hard to accomplish later, to compare it, it is like water moves by the wind and the light of the flower moves by the dew.

Finally, I would like to present an essay by SGI President Ikeda.

Happy marriage

It is not easy to say how a husband and wife should behave towards each other. Sometimes the situation develops in a strange way, so that a leisurely and peaceful marriage may be absurdly divided, and sometimes in other people's eyes there may be difficult problems piled up like mountains, but in inside their marriage relationship can allow the two to get closer and share the happiest time.

True love, which can be said to be a strong bond between the two, is a love that has been gradually grown in the rough secular world. However, it doesn't mean that one of two must always yield or has to suffer for the sake of the other's satisfaction.

Marriage is not concentrating on a husband or wife. It is not a relationship that another person should be sacrificed for the success and happiness of the other person whichever of the two who becomes the leader. Marriage means playing musical instruments with each other's unique personality, just as a good song harmonizes lyrics and notes, playing a life melody together at the same time.

If you ask the secret of a happy marriage, is how to make the beautiful song with helping each other as a life partner. And the two important factors for developing a deep and harmonious marriage is the purpose of life which can be shared and feeling grateful for each other.

I don't know if I can compare a family to an airplane in today's society. Pilot and co-pilot must agree on the destination in order to ensure that the plane can reach its destination safely and that the plane can remain stable during the flight, and furthermore to be a successful flight.

Love comes in a thousand shapes. Even a husband who is unable to maintain a good relationship with others can

About Nietzscheanism

create an amazing harmony as a couple. On the other hand, there is a wife who does everything on her way. However, even in that marriage, there may be felt the harmonious atmosphere as a couple.

The following is the story of a couple.

After a long period of frustration, she finally fell into bed, and her sick life became her daily life. One day a doctor, who was familiar with her and her husband, handed her a prescription note through her husband. When she unfolded the prescription paper written by the doctor, she was very shocked. It was said like this.

"When your husband gives you the medicine, say 'Thank you' three times in a clear tone to your husband and then take the medicine."

She had a strange feeling about this. But because she had to follow the doctor's instructions, she must say "Thank you" to her husband three times before taking the medicine each time.

One day, she becomes aware of herself, who has forgotten this word for a long time. Each time she repeated "Thank you" three times, her health and happiness began to sprout.

The humble attitude of expressing gratitude makes not only the mind but also the appearance beautiful. Needless to say, this lesson applies equally to husbands.

Modest people have a humble mind. The mind of gratitude gives birth to being moved, touched and is to be the source of happiness.

In the English proverb, there is this word.

"Keep your eyes wide open before marriage, and half shut afterward."

Part 7

The last battle

No philosopher is read as much as Nietzsche, and no philosopher is widely misread. It is said that there are no people who don't know Nietzsche, and there are no people who know Nietzsche correctly.

Nietzsche is by no means humble. It is seen as arrogant But there is a dignity in it. The core subject he was trying to talk about was what he wrote in a literary narrative.

Nietzsche did not systematically provide his ideas. He didn't even make a demonstration. Instead, he urged readers persistently to think and act together. In addition, his argument is one-sided and highly declarative. There is room for a counterargument, but the opportunity for counterargument doesn't exist.

Nietzsche's ideas are like a maze. Criticism has always been followed that it is disorganized and fool of paradox. There are many people who are enthusiastic about him and also people who are opposed to him. The choice is up to readers, whether to accept or reject him.

Why would he do that?

The reason is surprisingly simple.

Nietzsche wanted his philosophy to be completed as a religion. He hoped that his philosophy would penetrate human life and transform it from the bottom up. So if his way was realized, he hoped that a new horizon would open up in the human world, and water would fill the new sea, and the sun would rise again. In other words, he kept in mind the religious revolution.

Nietzsche, who was more proud than anyone else, knew that what he understood with reason would be forgotten with time, and he did not want his philosophy to be forgotten with time. He never wanted it to be left unfinished.

The reason to say so is the unusual breathing of him that any reader who has read his book will experience. Ending writing the 「Thus Spoke Zarathustra」, Nietzsche said confidently.

"I gave mankind the biggest gift ever, the largest of all. With a voice that will spread for thousands of years, it is the greatest and most profound book that exists in the world and has been born from the deepest treasure of truth, on which if using the bucket, the gold and good will be given inevitably. This book is a gospel that makes a man happy and a future Bible that delivers joy. For people to own my book, they must have the bravest fists with the softest fingers."

But the situation didn't go as Nietzsche wanted. It ran into a very different direction. Nietzsche had thought he could easily show us a way to acquire a free spirit, a way to become superhuman. In his thought, all he has to do was just showing us the way he walked, which was already his and certain way.

Nietzsche was confident that he had reached a fairly high level of enlightenment. In fact, he lived in a mysterious world called the "Buddhist commandments" after the process of self-conquest. Based on the experience he overcame, he elaborated the "method of performance" that ordinary people could also become like him.

Do your readers remember? Do you remember the important story that I briefly mentioned in the prologue, 'Ubermensch and Buddha nature'? Ubermensch is Buddha nature spoken in Buddhism. Buddha nature means the 'power of life' that supports everything alive with infinite vitality, infinite wisdom, and mercy. And when you apply Buddha nature to an individual, it becomes an inner power, Ubermensch, that can overcome you.

The task that Nietzsche was trying to accomplish risking everything was not something else, but something that calling the immortality that was sleeping in the deep side of human life. This is because he can become superhuman only if he calls Buddha nature. He was keeping on a tough fight to open the way that anyone could be superhuman. The problem was that the task of calling Buddha nature could not be done by just anyone.

Time passed and Nietzsche's contemplation and anguish deepened. In the meantime, three years have passed. But he was still wandering in the thick fog. He could hardly solve the problem. Eventually, Nietzsche was in the same circumstances as the soldier who was driven into an unknown war.

To be exact, despite his bitter struggle of three years and four months, Nietzsche ends up not being able to show us the way of practicing asceticism. Then, he looks up at the sky and kneeled down, lamenting the limitations of his abilities. Thus, the way of practicing asceticism in which anyone can be superhuman existed permanently in his heart without showing it to the world. What was the problem?

Generally speaking, the role is divided into two when the great religious revolution takes place. A theory is presented first, followed by practice.

The "Soka Renaissance" that marked the 21st century, the century of life, in which human emerges as the master of life, isn't an exception. Nietzsche took charge of the theory and Ikeda took charge of the practice.

As mentioned in "The Last Pattern of Life," when the heavenly value collapses, humans are forced to come down to earth and create new values to survive on this earth, and there are only two ways of living in this world. One is the way of life to be superhuman, and the other is the way of human living as the final or last human.

Humans struggle to protect themselves and live like humans in the last stream of last life like a swarm of poison flies, but they cannot help being desperate to look back at themselves as already being washed away in the mud. Despair leads to the death of the mind.

Human beings have only two choices. One is that depending

passively on 'the last way of life' as given, and another one is, the to be Ubermensch, superhuman and leading life into the positive direction.

Then how can we call Ubermensch?

All the flowers and trees that exist in this world grow with countless light and heat pouring from the sun. To call Buddha nature which is dormant in human life like that, a very strong light source is needed. Where on earth can I find that light source? Nietzsche's agony was just about this.

Regrettably, Nietzsche boundary Nietzsche entered was the world of best enlightenment, that is the world of Buddha, but not the boundary of True Buddha(本佛) in which he can send out countless lights to bring about disbelief and revive life. He was staying one step down from there. He was staying in the moon-like Buddha of traces(迹佛). Nietzsche never knew that truth.

Technically, there are two kinds of Buddha. True Buddha and the Buddha of traces are that. The True Buddha is the person who embodies extremely bright light like Sun, shining everywhere in this world. In detail, the life of the True Buddha is spreading the light to every life spread around the whole world, who can show the power of the Mother nature regenerating life, on his body. However, the Buddha of traces means that various Buddha from the three generations and the ten directions.

China's Yellow River purifies its own dirty water once a thousand years. Just like that, True Buddha also appears in the world once every 1,000 years to remove the dark clouds of human agony.

When a great evil(大惡) arrives, the great virtue(大善) follows, bringing hope and courage to human beings, thus reducing the weight of life. That is the strange reason for this world. The same was true in the case of Nietzsche.

The moment Nietzsche kneeled down looking up at the sky and lamenting the limitations of his abilities, he had a great realization. The realization was that when the great religious revolution took place, the role was necessarily divided into two, and through "Thus Spoke Zarathustra" he realized that he had already put forward a 'book of theories' for the religious revolution that was coming to the world. His role had been already finished long ago successfully.

Nietzsche, who felt easy in mind, in the next year (1888), published the works that he had written in his spare time.

Six works came at once like a violent storm. 「The Case of Wagner」, 「Twilight of the Idols」, 「The Antichrist」, 「Ecce Homo」, 「Nietzsche contra Wagner」, 「Hymn of Dionysus」are them.

In Nietzsche's last work, 「Ecce Homo」, he returns to his past and continues to boast about his work. 'Why I am so wise,' 'Why I am so clever,' 'Why I write such a good book,' and 'why I am one destiny.'

Here, however, the reader needs to understand why Nietzsche is flattering himself. As for Nietzsche, the state of his stage of enlightenment does not give much meaning to the joy, sorrow, pride, and lovable feelings that human generally feels, with those emotions being fainted. Instead, how I could accomplish what I want and the result of how much I was able to burn myself comes as a feeling of satisfaction before other emotions. In other words, Nietzsche's endless boasting may be the elaborated strategic work to appeal to the minds of readers.

Nietzsche's philosophy, called the flower of modern philosophy, was honored to play the role of lighting up the great religious revolution, 'Soka Renaissance'. The last regret of Nietzsche, the way of practicing asceticism to be superhuman will be presented by the SGI President Ikeda instead.

SGI President Ikeda says.

"Human well-being starts from fighting and winning against one's weak mind. Human revolution means winning from yourself.

If there's no hope now, you have to build your own hope. If you think you're unhappy now, you have to create your own happiness. First, you have to be the sun and expand the sunlight around you.

Just as vegetation is reaching for the sun, people are pursuing happiness. For a better life, for an improved life. It's a natural action of life.

Religion is the basis of human values and life, and according to what religion you believe in, human's happiness and unhappiness will be determined. Only when people learn knowledge and become wise will new period come.

Sunshine of the hope which eliminating the dark clouds of modern civilization is the law of life, the Buddhism. The great universe is inside the human mind which is the very object of the three thousand realms in a single moment of life(一念三千). The human has good, evil and unlimited possibility with a lively motion in a moment. But the absence of a philosophy of life that reveals the truth of man makes us distrust human beings, and that distrust pile up to be human division. This division is the biggest source of evil.

As a believer of Buddhism, our role is to inform the life philosophy, the unchanging value. Our role is significant in creating happiness.

This Buddhism(Lotus Sutra) of the great saint Nichiren, which established the dignity, equality, and freedom, is the true world religion itself, brightening 21st century's future and lightening up the happiness to the world. And it's the SGI movement that creates the history of human regeneration lightening the humanism for the people of the world in agony.

Great propagation of Buddhism is a religious revolution never existed. And religion is the basis of human society and the deepest soil. It is natural that when this revolution is achieved, it becomes a source of revolution throughout society. In the Latter Day of the Law, the primordial sun rose. The big light is enveloping everyone in the world."

Part 8

A picture of Mandara

Now we entered a period in which life is a keyword. Now the world is looking for something to revive a tired life in vitality. Where are the ideas, philosophies, and religions that answer it clearly?

Something is wrong. I need something. I'm also not happy with science. Nor can socialism or capitalism save me. No matter how much you hold meetings and appeal to morality, give lectures in psychology and discuss philosophy, it is not enough. Isn't this the true picture of the human mind?

Saint Exupery says, well known as the writer of 『The little prince』.

"We have to understand that we are on the wrong way some where. Humans have become richer in general than ever before. Enjoy more wealth and time. But there is a shortage of essentials that cannot be clearly defined. The incident of feeling me as human gradually becomes less and less. Something is missing from the precious things we have."

Contemporary time is the time in which all sorts of passions were abused and all idealism was broken. Young people should find idealism and passion, but young people already have no utopia in mind. In a word, the mood that dominates modern times is helplessness.

On the other side of this sense of helplessness is what Nietzsche calls a superhuman idea and an Ubermensch styled life. Nietzscheanism, in which man becomes the master of life, refers to the philosophy of life, the three thousand realms in a single moment of life(一念三千) in Lotus Sutra, and every one of us can be superhuman calling Ubermensch through 'practice of life', devotion(信心).

The Buddhist writings of three thousand realms in a single moment of life means literary that a human's determination changes everything, which is the life philosophy of teaching unlimited possibility and dignity of a human

In short, modern people are looking for something to fill the emptiness of mind sincerely. I'm looking for something to revive a tired life in vitality. They are eager for wisdom to teach them where to go and what society should do for them.

To live is to fight. Life is a struggle and society is a struggle.

Literary giant Goethe sang. "I was a human being. And that means he's a fighter."

What do we fight for? For one's own happiness. This is to build oneself that will never be frustrated no matter what happens. For the human revolution. To be superhuman.

Emerson, an American thinker, spoke clearly. "The will to serve others and contribute to the well-being of mankind, that is the essence of life."

The blue lake face also shines golden when the sun shines. Human also shines golden when the Buddhism's light shines. Human life changes depending on what standpoint of life and death you have.

Surprisingly, many people in the world want a new life. They want to be on the starting line again with their pounding hearts. And I can't wait to start, so I want to run and grab my life for sure. People are only doing their best today to complete the only life they have. Isn't that right?

The Soka Gakkai International, at after war(the World War

2), started from almost nothing to the 3,000 members when Josei Toda was appointed as the second President in 1951. In just 20 years, however, it has become Japan's largest religious organization with '10 million members'. Furthermore, the unknown people became the main leader of social construction, pushing for reforms in various fields such as culture, education, and politics, creating a great trend for the people. Indeed, it was so wonderful that it can be said as the 'miracle of modern times'.

How was it possible? The reason is quite simple. Because the members of the Soka Gakkai International were able to achieve their dreams through faith and religious belief. They say. "This religion is a living religion!" The phrase 'living' means that religion has power. This means that as much as one is sincere to faith, the results can always appear in real life. So how could they enjoy their faith and also get the virtue they wanted?

Now, let me briefly tell you about 'The Object of worship(御本尊)' that SGI members support.

The Object of worship is the essence of their faith. The original site is 'a width of Mandara', enshrined in the Buddhist altar of each family. The Mandara is not the painting but characters written in bold letters.

Nichiren, the True Buddha of the Latter Day of the Law wrote his soul using ink, the principle is that if you list up the things to be dealt toward Object of worship, the Buddha will realize in the person of listing up the things to be dealt. It's rare, but when we read a good and great book, we can sometimes feel the author's soul breathing in it because it contains life. Likewise, when the things to be dealt with is given to Object of worship, Buddha nature rises from the one who is giving the things to be dealt with.

As a result of the rising of Buddha nature, the surrounding area is also brightened. Brightening the surrounding area means that everything you want is going in the right direction. Many forms of good and pleasant things that you experience through faith are called virtues. That virtues include both spiritual and material side.

Inside Object of worship of SGI members, "Nam-myoho -renge-ko(南無妙法蓮華經)" is written in the middle in bold font. Nam-myoho-renge-ko means the power of the fundamental universe or the truth and refers to Lotus Sutra. The wonderful law they refer to means the power of Mother Nature reviving life by sending light to all life in the whole universe.

SGI members post the things to be dealt towards this Object of worship. Posting the things to be dealt refers to saying 'Nam-myoho-renge-ko' repeatedly. They make their wishes to the

Object of worship, and when their wishes come true, they become more courageous and devote themselves to their faith.

Ando Shusaku, a prominent Japanese writer, wrote many works of Christian religious literature, which he says in his book. "Every human has a deep sense of longing for God. Even if it's not God, it is an absolute thing, a desire to find one's true nature."

But he avoids mentioning about how to find true nature. In a broad sense, it can be said that the reason for a man's search for religion is his desire to find himself, his true nature, as he says.

And given that he is a Christian, he may have wanted to say that man can find his nature by getting close to God. On the other hand, he says, "Even if it is not God, we can find human's true nature through the absolute thing."

The absolute thing that he says, which is the wonderful law, unchanging law of life, or the truth. And every human being wants to know the truth, and when he finds the light of the possibility of seeing the truth, life becomes full of energy. But on the contrary, when the light of the possibility is lost, darkness spreads upon an empty mind. It is because human nature is with the very truth.

SGI President Ikeda says.

"To receive the Gohonzon(御本尊) means to receive the body of the Buddha. Object of worship is hanging on our mind, too. The deep will lies in believing Object of worship is ourselves.

The Object of worship covers the entire universe. Therefore, a person who believes in Object of worship and posts the things to be dealt can have a good life calmly and peacefully. Through faith, we can lead a wonderful life without fail in the wonderful law.

Reading the scriptures of Buddhism is a magnificent ceremony. With doing this act of Buddhist commandments on and on, I can make my Buddhahood solid like unshakable land.

Faith may seem weak at first glance, but it is actually the most powerful force in the world.

The action of the Devil and the Buddha exists together in our lives. After all, it's a fight of yourself. Whether in Buddhist-Dharma practice, in social work, in history, in politics, in economic growth, everything boils down to basically a battle of good and evil.

Winning in life is not an outward form. It has nothing to do with the vanity of showing off to others. Ultimately, victory in life depends on how serious you actually fight and move forward.

The purpose of faith is to be happy. Hopefully, all of you will take this certain way leading to happiness. We should never wander off on the path leading to misfortune. With conviction and pride, walk into a great way of great propagation of Buddhism.

Because humans live under the grace of nature, saving nature leads to protecting the human. The sense of gratitude, the sense of consciousness, the emotion of joy, leads to greater happiness.

Love comes in a thousand shapes. Like that, faith appears in a thousand different ways. When you pray with gratitude, your pray combines with the rhythms of the great universe's rhythm to change your life into a good direction.

The 'Soka Renaissance' pursued by SGI is an unknown religious revolution. And religion is the deepest soil that forms the basis of human society. The wonderful law is the power of Mother Nature, which brings light to all life in the whole universe and resuscitates it.

There is nothing in the world that a person who has mastered the wonderful law(Nam-myoho-renge-ko) can't overcome. Sunshine of Hope eliminating dark clouds is the very law of life, Buddhism.

The human revolution brings a change in real life, the flowers of virtue and produce the fruits of happiness. The person who cried the most in misfortune has the right to be the happiest.

A new era has arrived. The period of singing and dancing have passed and the period of philosophy seeking truth came. Having a goal in life means having hope. It becomes the light of youth and the power of life.

The great propagation of Buddhism is the noblest channel of gold from the Latter Day of the Law that we live in, to the future for the eternal prosperity of mankind. Let's march on this path bravely and boldly, as the teachings of the great saint Nichiren. This is the surest way to achieve world peace.

If we don't spread the Buddhism of the great saint Nichiren, there will be no hope for human happiness and peace."

Now, here I want to introduce you to a passage from writings of the great saint Nichiren.

"As one character of Lotus Sutra is like the great land, it gives birth to everything, as one character is like the great sea, it embraces every people, as one character is like days and months, it shines the four worlds(四天下). How your pray will not be achieved. Even if someone points the great land and fails, and even if someone exists who is tieing empty space, and even if come and go of the tide doesn't exist, and even if the sun rises from the West, there will not exist the thing of not achieving the pray of the practitioner of Lotus Sutra."

The 'practitioner of Lotus Sutra' in this passage doesn't mean special existence. It means general believers. It means the people who abide by the belief purely as Buddha said. As everything's reason is alike, how much purely and seriously the person prays makes the result changes.

There is a treasure called one wish jewel. Although its size is like the mustard seed, it gives a ten thousand of treasures. It is an ethereal bead that makes everything in his mind.

When Charles Lee takes a conversation with others, he often compares One Wish Jewel to Object of worship of his belief. The reason for his proud saying is that he prayed everything he wanted to Object of worship and truly achieved it.

He is enjoying the joy of belief as much as he likes.

Contemporary people bearing everyday life with the mind of departing to somewhere. I'd like to suggest this 'a breadth of Mandara'.

Nietzscheanism is completed by SGI this way

Part 9

Doctor Toynbee

Seattle was a beautiful city surrounded by the sea and moun tains. Elliott Bay's hill is spread up to around the coast of the Pacific Ocean, and over the forest, Rainier Mt. which is similar to the Mount Fuji, was shining like silver.

Because the lake Washington, Seattle's attraction is con nected to the sea and canal, the sluice gate for controlling the water level. The sluice gate was closed and a ship came and went. Ikeda President and his company watched that view, and the drizzle rained. On the opposite side of the lake, yellow and red colored leaves were spread like watercolor wet with thin fog drip.

"Beautiful, Such a beautiful scene! It is like a picture. However, I cannot but to feel vanity thinking that this beauty will soon go away."

Kiyohara told sentimentally. Then Ikeda replied her saying smiling silently.

"Red autumn colors, maybe it is the figure of leaves living within limited time burning itself as much as it could. Everything is in vanity. A human cannot avoid birth, old age, sickness, and death. So, there is no way but to perform one's mission. Life is the fighting with limited time. The thing that I need now is the time to accomplish that mission."

His final word contained his urgent mind. However, nobody understood his innermost feelings at the bottom. In his mind, the oath of Great propagation of Buddhism was burning in the color of cherry red like the maple tree of this autumn

Eventually, the primitive sun rose with brilliant light. The primitive sun was rising to get rid of the darkness of every distrust and hatred and to send the light of peace which is the wish of mankind. That light of hope was reaching everywhere of an abyss of sorrow and despair without any sound changing the land of the human with the whirlpool of suffering into the flower garden of the delight. Nobody couldn't obstruct this rising sun.

Early October 1960.

Daisaku Ikeda 3rd Presiden of the Soka Gakkai International, 32 years old.

He was leaving to the world burning the fire of auto to himself for the contribution to the peace of mankind. It was only after 5 months of his appointment of President. That day, the autumn sky of Tokyo was spread in blued endless.

His overseas visiting was making the breakthrough of the today's SGI(Soka Gakkai International) movement which shines the light of humanism to the world people in agony, making the history of the mankind recover.

This drama of the human revolution received attention slowly as time passed. It was surprisingly the Western intellectuals that showed the interest of the 'Soka Renaissance' which is on one side can be seen as a revolution of the religion.

For them who have lived with religion as a basis of life, the number of reasons for the interest of Soka Gakkai International was 2 generally. First reason was that this revolution of religion was developed through not by clerics but by people, and the second reason was that this revolution of religion was that this revolution of religion bear in mind that the religion of the world which can replace the Christianity which is losing power in the

Nietzscheanism is completed by SGI this way

West, as to say the to be the higher religion.

Kuwabara Dakeo(Kyoto University's honorary professor) who translated the 『Study of History』 By the history scholar Toynbee, told later from that time.

"Unlike Japan in which the religion lost power because of the power of politics, the intellectuals of the West have much interest on the Soka Gakkai International much more than the intellectuals of Japan. Toynbee was one of them."

Autumn, 1969

President Ikeda received a letter written by the typewriter. The letter of Dr. Toynbee. It was the first letter of the history scholar of mankind representing the 20th century. He read the translated letter with a pounding heart.

"1967, when I was in Japan for the last time, I heard the story of Soka Gakkai International and you.

- Omitted -

I'm really interested in your ideas or writings. So, if you are fine, I'd like to invite you for us two to exchange opinions regarding many problems encountered by current mankind."

The background of Dr. Toynbee's strong wish of the conversation with President Ikeda was that he had a special interest in

Buddhism as a higher religion which can overcome the crisis of the modern civilization of mankind. Dr. Toynbee's mind was led by the truth of Soka Gakkai International's achievements of the social building with reviving the philosophy of Buddhism in the contemporary period, and the SGI was actually born in the people.

Japan's religious organizations survived with opportunism with the authority. However, the Soka Renaissance carried forward the movement of the religion in the people's side to realize human's happiness holding the flag of the revolution of the religion by the spirit of the great saint Nichiren. Because of that 21 executives went to prison being the target of the military authorities, there were persecutions, for example, the 1st President, Makiguchi Tsunesaburo died in prison.

Also, in the postwar period, Soka Gakkai International developed the movement of social development in various areas such as politics, economics, education, art with the human revolution centered which is to revolutionize the human who is the main agent of every creation based on Buddhism. The expansion of this movement of religion which is mainly by the people meant the new force of people came to the force. Existing religions and the authority of many classes resisted furiously to the Soka Gakkai International in the fear.

President Ikeda wrote the reply in a polite manner.

"I received your letter in gratitude. I think it is the most meaningful chance in my life to meet the doctor that I admired the most from the past."

However, President Ikeda was really busy. At that moment he cannot say anything but to say that 'I'll try hard to realized your invitation'. President Ikeda's health was bad from the end of 1969. Furthermore, he was really busy with the opening of a Soka(Soka Gakkai) University ahead in 1971.

Since then the Doctor requested the conservation with President Ikeda incessantly. The doctor showed the intention of going to Japan by himself if President Ikeda is hard to come to England. However, it was hard for the old man to travel for a long time. President Ikeda decided that at the next year of the opening of Soka University, he will certainly visit England in the correspondent to the invitation of the Doctor.

May, 4th, 1972. Finally, President Ikeda and his company departed Orly Airport of Paris. The airplane arrived in London after 1 hour over the Strait of Dover. London street was full of green colored trees and beautiful flowers blowing in the breeze.

In the morning of the next day, Dr. Ikeda and his company went to the house of Dr. Toynbee by car. His house was 20 minutes from London in a sequestered residential area. Eventually, the car stopped in front of the house of Dr. Toynbee. President and his company stepped out of the car.

"Oh, Mr. Ikeda! Mrs. Ikeda! It is my pleasure of you visiting far away here!"

The Doctor bent oneself who is tall put out his hand. President Ikeda held that hand strongly. It was a long-awaited moment. Toynbee couple showed everywhere inside the house such as a library. The household was not splendid at all.

The doctor sat on the sofa and putting up the white hair carelessly and looked President Ikeda's face directly. And he said nodding many times.

"I waited. I waited."

President Ikeda also stared the face of the Doctor. Hearing aid in the ear. He was known as suffering from heart disease. However, brilliant eyes were shining in the strong light of belief over the glasses. Even it was the first meeting, it felt like the reunion maybe because they shared many times already. The great scholar's honest aspect was really warm.

Nietzscheanism is completed by SGI this way

President Ikeda went on.

"There are many problems to be worried and solved being regarded as the question of the human in the turbulent human world. I really wished to listen to the Doctor's opinion regarding these matters. It will be much happier than my expectation if this conversation can give clue to solve problems for the many people who will live the 21st century."

Doctor Toynbee said with flushed face and shining eyes.

"I also think everything in the focus of the upcoming centuries. How will the future go? Even after me and you, how the world will change? I have a deep interest in this."

The Doctor's eyes were looking really long future. The human living in the present has the responsibility to build the future. President Ikeda told.

"I, as the Buddhist philosopher, researched fundamental things like 'What is the dignity of the life' or 'What is the human'. I'd like to talk about this matter intensively."

"Yes, Yes, Yes."

The Doctor nodded many times with a smile. And told in a resolute attitude.

"Actually I wanted to talk about that matter. I waited long for this chance. Let's do this! Let's talk about the 21st century more!

I will do my best."

It was a voice with such a strong resolution for an 80-year-old person. The two had lunch checking the schedule and the theme of the conversation. The Doctor invited President Ikeda's company to the French restaurant.

The historic conversation started at 3 p.m.

Doctor Toynbee and President Ikeda sit on the sofa with their back to the window. Kaneko and madam Veronica were also with them. The conversation went on in style of the question of President Ikeda and the answer of the Doctor.

President Ikeda firstly asked in the big subject of 'What the human being is.' There was no uncomfortable thing because of formality. The mood was warm. However, it struck on a rock when the story was about the convoluted subjects like the theory of life or the philosophy of history.

Three people were an amateur as a translator. It was hard to translate deep and philosophic stories. Even, the Doctor's vocabulary was really extensive and the logic was really complex. Even though President Ikeda always thought that he needs a competent translator, this was the most urgent.

The first day's conversation was active including the

Nietzscheanism is completed by SGI this way

philosophy of history, the theory of study and theory of art and also the theory of life. There was a problem of translation, it was happy to get much fruition.

6th, May, which is the next day, President Ikeda and his wife Kaneko invited Doctor Toynbee couple in lunch. It was Japanese cuisine. They pleasantly talked about the character and culture of Japan. President Ikeda asked.

"What is your favorite food among Japanese food?"

"I like everything. Sushi is my best pick. My wife doesn't like that much..."

Toynbee who visited Japan three times told he likes to eat packed lunch sold in the subway. There was a story that once his companion was shocked because he ate everything of the packed lunch.

The Doctor harmonized to the different culture even if he visits anywhere. The first step may be the experience of local food culture without prejudice. After lunch, the conversation went on in the Doctor's house.

"What is the thing you want to do most now?"

"The thing that I'm doing now. This conversation means the effort to united the whole world into one family. I think for mankind's survival, the whole humanity needs to be one big family."

President Ikeda asked again.

"What do you want to be if you are born again."

The Doctor said in a silent tone with a lonely smile.

"I'm reluctant to be born as human again. It is because humans are to be unhappy existence than any other animals. Well, I became pessimistic."

And went on like muttering.

"... I want to be a bird. The bird in India. It is because Indians think human rights in creatures other than humans."

The doctor did not speak of complacent optimism about the future of mankind. The sharp eyes would be penetrating the grave crisis in human history. Ikeda felt the mind of the doctor seriously. He made up his mind.

'I'll definitely make it. The future of humans that the Doctor can hope for!'

It was the last day of the talk, May 9th.

The main themes of the day were the theory of happiness, suicide problem, Oriental medicine, and Buddhism. As the talks ended, Ikeda asked.

"You are a life's huge senior of life. Please let me know if you have any advice for future generations. First of all, what should 10s and 20s young people have to keep in mind for the 21st century?"

The doctor answered at once.

"Tough patience. And I'd like to say, in particular, to avoid violence."

Ikeda felt the same way. His former teacher, what Josei Toda mentioned as the first thing among the fight that young people do was also "to wear the armor of patience(忍辱)" In this context, patience means the endurance of insult or persecution. patience is the source of every achievement of greatness.

At 5:30 p.m., Ikeda finished the question.

There was still a lot he wanted to ask the Doctor. There were also many questions to answer. But the appointment was due that day. So we decided to exchange questions or answers with letters. And they promised to meet again someday.

said Mrs. Veronica, regrettably.

"It's a nice day, so let's take a walk in the park together for a while."

Everyone agreed. The doctor went out with a hat on and a coat on. He was also an English gentleman. It was evening, but it was still bright outside. The wind was fresh. Surrounded by a thick green forest, the park was inhabited by small birds and wild animals.

Ikeda took the doctor's left arm and moved slowly. The other arm was supported by Kawasaki. The doctor spoke with a note of excitement.

"My long-cherished wish has come true. I was able to have a really meaningful conversation. Mr. Ikeda, I improve when I talk to you. I'm touched. I think we've discussed important issues with each other. It was the most valuable time. As a scholar, there is no more joy."

"Thank you. I'm so impressed to hear valuable words."

"You said an important question about human life. And it's not idealism, but full of passion to get to the essence to solve the problems of reality. I can organize my own studies through this talk."

There is a detonation of a soul in a true conversation. Conversation is the mother of creation. The doctor stared President Ikeda's face and said in a strong voice:

"Let's continue our conversation. Can you come to my house again?"

"Yes, I'll be glad to see you."

"Oh, Thank you very much!"

Nietzscheanism is completed by SGI this way

The doctor took Ikeda's hand and began to walk as if he were dancing on the steps. From the surrounding woods, birds sang and flew into the wide sky.

A year has passed since him.

In May 1973, the two men's talks resumed at Dr. Toynbee's house. In the last year's talk, Ikeda usually asked questions and the doctor answered them, but this time, the doctor asked many questions. The focus was especially on the role of religion.

The doctor pointed out that the causes of many evils that would destroy humanity, such as nuclear weapons and environmental destruction, are greed and aggression in humans, and it starts from self-centered tendencies.

"The modern threat to human survival can only be eliminated by the revolutionary transformation that takes place in the minds of every human being. And this transformation of mind must be developed into religion to give birth to the willpower needed to bring new ideal into practice."

The doctor had huge hopes for the 'human revolution movement' organized by the Soka Gakkai International. Dr. Toynbee grew up in a Christian family but has studied religion objectively and thus explored its original attitude. In his book, 「An Historian's Approach to Religion」 the reason why Christianity has become widespread is explained.

The doctor first noted that Christians have fulfilled all the duties of citizens and acted as good citizens, unless they are opposed to conscience, while resolutely enduring persecution. Furthermore, he noted that Christianity captured the hearts of the public. Then why could Christianity capture the hearts of the masses? The doctor cited three reasons.

First, because Christians treated the public not only as workers but as human beings with souls. Second, Christians extended the hand of relief to wives, orphans, patients and old people who had lost their husbands, who had almost no care from the city-state or the government of the empire. Thirdly, he wrote that all this was because they did not have the will to gather supporters and abandoned self-interest as Christian ideology ordered.

In other words, the public has found hope in Christianity, as Christians have made all their efforts for the public more than anyone else. Christianity, which in its early days created a solid foundation, was broadened instantly. What can we do for the people? Therefore, the future of the nation and religion will be decided. However, as it enters the age of 17, Christianity

Nietzscheanism is completed by SGI this way

once worked hard for people to make the basis of development started to show a tendency to decline.

Dr. Toynbee and Ikeda were bold even to talk about the later modern West.

Ikeda stressed.

"Religion has always been a source of civilization and a driving force for creativity, whereas since modern times Western civilization is seen as a non-religious civilization, which is based on the departure from religion. But if you go one step further and expand the concept of 'religion', modern science and technology civilization has its own 'civilization'. For example, the desire for material wealth, the progressive belief in science, has become the 'religion' of modern people?

"I totally agree," he said, adding that the void of Christianity in the West was filled with the three new 'religions'. It was called 'faith in scientific progress' and 'nationalism' and 'communism'. But the advances in science led to atomic bombs, nationalism led to wars, and communism fell into irrelevance and exclusiveness, and these religions were concluded as, "Among them, nothing can be satisfied."

The doctor stressed.

"So I felt I needed a new kind of religion. I have a question about what the future religions of humanity are."

The condition of 'future religion' presented by the doctor was that "it should now be to give mankind the power to overcome all the evils that seriously threaten the survival of mankind."

Furthermore, he mentioned what 'all evil' is, that the religion has to solve, which brings and supports new civilization. He noted that 'It is an artificial environment created by man using science to satisfy his desires', 'war and social injustice', and 'greed that always follows life'.

The conversation has finally reached a climax. Ikeda said step by step that religion that overcame what Dr. Toynbee said was Buddhism.

"Greed is a matter of the inside of human beings, war or social discrimination is a matter of human versus human, or of the dimension of society, and environmental destruction is a problem arising from human versus natural relationships. These three categories of self-social-environment have been declared as Between three worlds(三世間) in Buddhism."

After saying so, Ikeda stressed that it is the law of Buddhism that mentioned the words of inseparable relationship and connection in the deep dimension of the social environment surrounding humans and the natural environment.

Nietzscheanism is completed by SGI this way

The doctor nodded his head widely. And said it in a declarative manner.

"A right religion is a religion that teaches us to be noble about the dignity and sanctity of the whole nature, including humans and other things besides humans. By comparison, wrong religions allow humans to satisfy their own greed at the expense of nature other than humans."

Ikeda went on to discuss what the Buddhism is.

"Buddhism is a religion based on the laws of life widely existing between nature's between the universe and all human beings. In other words, the core of Buddhism is the integration of the fundamental laws inherent in the universe and human life, and from there, it is revealed that humans have a way to integrate and cooperate with nature."

The doctor said.

"I knew what I had just heard about the characters of Buddhism. That reminds me of what I mean by higher religion. When I say higher religion, it means a religion that makes each human being directly connected to 'the ultimate spiritual reality'."

'The ultimate spiritual reality' symbolized the doctor's view of religion. There is a spiritual presence in the universe which is greater than human beings themselves. It is the human purpose to harmonize the 'ultimate reality' behind the cosmic phenomenon, the doctor has argued from the old days. In Dr. Toynbee's opinion, religion, by which 'the ultimate reality' can only be contacted by clerics can never become a higher religion.

Ikeda also thought that religion should directly connect people to 'the ultimate reality'. It is because each person should be the main character. Ikeda, therefore, decided that he would never allow for the tyranny of clerics blocking the people, with the clothes of authority on his body.

The two men's opinion regarding higher religion was the same. President Ikeda stressed.

"There is no doubt that today is the moment which needs a higher religion which has that meaning. I think the basic challenge to get deeper and deeper is the question of what their religion is based on. As to say, higher religion is all about 'in the basis of god' or 'on the basis of law'. I think only this kind of religion can withstand the hardships of rational thought as well as overcome and lead."

The doctor analyzed that humans are looking for 'the ultimate reality' in only human things. However, he suggested that

Nietzscheanism is completed by SGI this way

human is also a part of nature, and to make the human, which is a part of nature, as a god and making it as 'the ultimate reality' is also irrational. And he concluded.

"I think the legal system of universal life in Buddhism is showing the 'the ultimate reality of mentality' more flawlessly."

Ikeda stressed that 'the law' inherent in life in space is 'the ultimate reality' and that 'the law' is the root of all the rules that cause and maintain a strong harmony between the phenomena of the universe. The Doctor listened to that story carefully with shining eyes. It was the opening the eyes(開眼) to the wonderful law(妙法) of the universe's root.

In many ways, Ikeda had a disagreement with the doctor, so he thought that there would be times when their opinions are not the same. Most of the time, however, the two had a consensus. In particular, in the opinion that selfish 'small-self' should be united to the 'big-self(大我, Ubermensch)' for the 'self-overcome', which can be said as the purpose of the religion, they perfectly agreed.

It was time to say goodbye.

The conversation between the two has been around 40 hours, including talks in May last year. In there farewell, Dr. Toynbee held Ikeda's hand and said:

"I think conversation plays a huge role in bringing together civilizations, peoples and religions around the world. I hope you to open more of these conversations to unite the entire human race."

The words rang in Ikeda's heart like a mission entrusted by a doctor.

"All right, I promise. We'll expand the wave of conversation to the world until I die."

Their eyes glowed at each other. Ikeda politely thanked the Doctor and Mrs. Veronica.

"Thank you. You've given me a lot of valuable advice for the future of humanity. Your conversation is the most valuable asset of my life. Thank you very much."

Dr. Toynbee hugged President Ikeda, and Mrs. Veronica hugged Kaneko feeling sorrow of farewell. The doctor and his wife looked them out. After shaking hands with the Doctor several times, Ikeda got into the car.

"Thank you very much!"

President Ikeda yelled shaking his hand. The Doctor couple shook hands endlessly. That scene was remembered in his mind forever like a famous painting.

Nietzscheanism is completed by SGI this way

Part 10

San Francisco

Five and a half hours after the departure of Honolulu, over the horizon, there was a pale mist melting in the sky, and all over the country was connected to the U.S. mainland. Ikeda looked down at the continent stretching out of the window. Underneath the bay was a wide stretch of urban land, and at the front of it, a red bridge of the Golden Gate Bridge was raised in the sunset. It's San Francisco.

Several members of the Soka Gakkai were in the lobby of the airport.

"Ikeda Sensei! Welcome. It's very nice of you to come."

A lady greeted Joo-jo, who was a vice-chairman. Although she already watched the picture of Ikeda in the Seiko newspaper, the weekly Soka Gakkai magazine, she thought

Joo-jo was the chairman because she didn't know who was the chairman. Ju-ju blushed and pointed to Ikeda, saying, "This is Ikeda Sensei!" The accompanying executives couldn't stand the funny situation of his embarrassing look.

"Oh, I'm sorry!"

Because of the mistake of Joo-jo misunderstanding him as Ikeda, the woman bowed her head over and over again.

"It's okay. you've never met me, so I understand. Thank you for coming to see me like this."

Ikeda smiled and comforted her and headed together to the waiting room at the airport. As soon as he entered the waiting room, Masaki introduced members. Yukiko Gilmore, who was first introduced, was a woman who played a central role in San Francisco.

Gilmore attended the Soka Gakkai International in Yokohama five years ago and came to the United States with her American husband the following year. Her health was so bad at that time that she had to go to the hospital endlessly in Japan, and after starting the faith, her health was recovered. Gilmore found Japanese-Americans in San Francisco and expanded the boundaries of the broadband religion.

Ikeda guessed her hardships talking to Yukiko Gilmore in

Nietzscheanism is completed by SGI this way

two or three words. He praised and encouraged her, who had struggled with all she got.

"It was hard, right? Thank you. But it's okay now."

At this moment, Gilmore's eyes watered.

President Ikeda spoke to a Japanese-American woman who stood hesitantly behind Gilmore. She looked tired of living and miserable.

"Your name?"

"I'm Ai Lynn."

"Come on, sit this way."

He offered her a chair. Ai Lynn was very nervous. Her husband was working in the U.S. military, and they were so poor, suffering from huge debts from gambling. When she heard the Buddhism story in June last year, she joined the Soka Gakkai International with a desire to catch straws.

"Are you doing faith hard?"

"Yes, I'm doing a 'faith like fire'!"

She said it in a simple manner. She has been taught that 'faith like fire' is a belief that goes off instantly even if a temporary fire breaks out, and 'faith like water' that continues like water is a strong faith's attitude. However, she answered the question wrong because she was so excited to answer as the 'faith like fire' was great.

"Oh, it's the opposite! I've never taught you that."

Yukiko Gilmore protested by holding onto Ai Lynn's sleeves. Ikeda smiled sweetly at Ai Lynn and said,

"'Faith like fire' is not to be taken. But you must be happy if you carry on your 'faith like water'!"

It was a word of conviction. At the word the thick cloud of sorrow that had engulfed Ai Lynn's heart was gone. He also spoke to the woman beside Yukiko Gilmore.

"Your name?"

"Yes, this is Kiyoko Taylor. In Japan, I was the group leader of the Kamata chapter."

"Was it the Kamata chapter? I miss it. Do you know my wife, then?"

"Yes, she has come to the meeting several times with her children. In addition, the first meeting I attended was at your wife's family, Haruki's house."

"Really? The world is small. But what about your husband?

"This is my husband. His name is Paul and he is a federal auditor."

She pointed to a big American who was beside her. And she added.

Nietzscheanism is completed by SGI this way

"But he doesn't do faith now. However, there is a cheering up."

He answered at once.

"Isn't that enough? It's already a great comrade for you to come and meet with us."

"Konnichiwa(Hello)!"

Then Paul Taylor greeted him in a poor Japanese with a bright smile.

"Oh, how do you do? I'm glad to hear that. It's nice of you coming here. I look forward to your kind cooperation."

Ikeda shook hands with Paul Taylor saying English also with his arms wide open. Gilmore's husband, who was standing on one side, also approached him and asked for a handshake. He was a man named Daniel, who had a nice face.

The two were so cheerful and impressionable Americans. President Ikeda gave Paul Taylor a medal to celebrate his appointment as President, who is not yet a member. Taylor then immediately put the medal on his neck and boasted it with open chests.

It was a bright and amicable welcome, quite different from when they arrived at Honolulu Airport in Hawaii, where they visited two days ago. President and his company headed for the hotel from the airport.

Ikeda attended the meeting, which began from 6:30 p.m
that day. There was a special guest room for them. Before the
meeting began, he invited some of the key local members to a
special guest room.

"Actually we're going to build a chapter in San Francisco
today. So I'd like to ask Yukiko Gilmore to be the chapter leader
and Jiyoko Taylor to be the woman chapter leader."

The two accepted with a nervous look. Then he told the two
husbands.

"Daniel and Paul, please be the chapter's advisers. Please
cheer for your wife as you do now and be a good person to talk
to with members of the chapter. May I ask you a favor?"

His words were translated by Masaki, who was beside
them. The two Americans said yes with a friendly nod, but
the executives from Japan couldn't hide their expressions of
surprise. Gilmore seems to have little knowledge of the deep
Buddhism, and Taylor has yet to register to the Soka Gakkai
International. The idea of setting the two men up as advisers
were beyond anyone's imagination.

Ikeda immediately said after being aware of the feelings of

Nietzscheanism is completed by SGI this way

the accompanying members.

"I want to cherish a man like Mr. Paul. He understands and cooperates well with the Soka Gakkai International even though he is not doing faith yet. There's no way I would like to pay the greatest thanks to the eager figure. You guys tend to judge a person by the faith and you become nervous or relieved. But that's wrong. Such a mindset is not the Buddhism.

There are many good people who are not religious but who have good character. If you look at the way such people live, there is a connection with the fundamentals of Buddhism. Therefore, if you judge a man to be a good man and a bad man by doing faith or not, you'll make a big mistake. No, I think it even causes human rights problems."

There was no wall between SGI and society in his thinking. It is the happiness of all and the peace of the world that we should hope as a Buddhist, as long as it is the Buddhism, as to say the society. It's as a large mountain with a wide foot does not easily collapse, but a cliff is so fragile.

Likewise, to accomplish Great propagation of Buddhism like a stable stone, the existence of around people who support SGI from various social perspectives is to be extremely important, such as the foot of a big mountain. Furthermore, he felt that such a friend's presence was a good example of the rightness of 'religion for human'.

By the beginning of the meeting, about 30 people attended the meeting. Most of them were Japanese women and surprised by a large number of people. Ai Lynn said in a small voice to Yukiko Gilmore.

"That's great! I can't believe so many people are here... I once heard the 'Bodhisattva of the Earth', and maybe did it rise from the Earth?"

"Don't say anything strange. Yesterday, you proudly told Ikeda that you were doing 'faith like fire' and he thinks I was teaching you something weird."

The two women's conversation was also heard in Ikeda's ears. He was gratified by such a naive conversation. Here in San Francisco, he was also asked questions. The question was always about the sadness of living in a foreign country where the language cannot be understood. He had to devote himself here too. Like firing a wet tree, he persuaded in the heart of embracement, and sometimes notified the greatness of Buddhism with fervent assurance.

He wiped the sweat off his forehead and carried on the story in a powerful voice.

"You have come to here San Francisco for a mission. Now each of you is struggling with great pain every day. However, it's all to prove the great force of Buddhism. You are the great pioneer of Great propagation of Buddhism in the U.S.A. Please note that all future U.S.A. is on your shoulders.

In that sense, I ask you three things today. First, be a good U.S. citizen by obtaining citizenship. Even the Great propagation of Buddhism, it is determined by how much trust the people get who push it. If you are in the United States and live like grass without root, thinking that you will return to Japan without loving even the country you are in, you cannot gain the trust of society. To acquire citizenship is to have the duty, responsibility, and rights to bear the country. That's the first step in building trust in society.

Secondly, please get a driver's license. Unlike Japan, the U.S. has a large territory. you need a car wherever you go. If you think about the widespread of Great propagation of Buddhism, it can be possible as much as you've moved, getting a driver's license is an indispensable condition for starting a full-scale fight.

Thirdly, master English. If you are free to speak English, you will have more American friends and can communicate with many people. Broadband religion begins with exchanges with others and exchanges begin with dialogues. And the Buddhism is not only for Japanese. If you think of the Great propagation of Buddhism, one day you should be able to speak English for conferences and words of encouragement at meetings. The one who should be at the center is here."

He looked around the hall.

Some quietly nodded their heads, while others looked perplexed. There was also a woman who was facing each other. Maybe they can't imagine each other driving a car and speaking English freely. He read the members' minds and said again.

"You may think you're asked to do hard work, but only you are responsible for the Great propagation of Buddhism in the U.S.A. I'm sure some of you think it's too much for you to drive a car and speak English freely. But first, try and do it with the determination of 'I certainly can do it.' and 'let's do it.' because it is you. Aren't there many female drivers in the United States? It's common sense for women to drive cars in the United States. One day, Japan will be in a period like that. In that sense, please be a pioneer of Japanese women.

There is no way that you cannot speak English. Here, even a five-year-old child speaks English. Compared to English,

Nietzscheanism is completed by SGI this way

Japanese is a very difficult language because it contains even Chinese characters. But didn't you master the Japanese excellent?"

There was a laugh. The laugh blew away the heavy heart that was holding back and spurred hope. 'Yes, I can do it!' That kind of mind was coming into everyone's heart.

During his overseas visit, Daisaku Ikeda appealed at conferences in various parts of the U.S.A. That is why it became the 'Three Guides'.

Even after the meeting, most of the members refused to return home. Everyone was happy. There were tea, snacks, and gimbap(rolled rice), and the flowers of conversation bloomed on this side and the other side. Some asked for guidance from accompanying executives, and some exchanged addresses.

He went back to the special guest room and was taking a rest when Mrs. Kiyohara came to see him.

"Sensei!"

said Kiyohara hesitantly.

"Well, actually Yukiko Gilmore and the members have collected a dollar each to serve us a meal..."

His face became dark when he heard Kiyohara.

"It can't be done!"

He called Yukiko Gilmore. And he taught well.

"I'm glad and grateful to your mind. But maybe all of you have a hard life now. We shouldn't, and don't have to burden everyone. And when I hear that I've decided to raise money to serve my meal, it creates an atmosphere that everyone has to follow, even if someone doesn't like it. Then it will be half-forcibly, even though it can be everyone's will, and distrust to the SGI can be made. This idea can be from the sincerity, but eventually, it can confuse everyone's faith.

Therefore, the leaders must refrain from making any careless money from the members. SGI is so strict in handling money that it's called neurotic. I think it's a little harsh, but please give it back to each person with explaining reasons."

Gilmore was at first embarrassed by his instruction, but then feeling like sorry, left the room, saying, "I understood you." He also knew that dining was an act that began for her good heart. It was sad to think that she needs to give everyone that money back with bowing her head. However, as a chapter leader, he cannot guarantee that one day she could fail because of money unless she is thoroughly familiar with SGI's financial problems. It was an instruction of mercy because of the thought for a comrade.

Nietzscheanism is completed by SGI this way

After a while, he put his face back on the place where the meeting had been held. Ai Lynn was busy carrying snacks and tea as she walked busily among the people in conversation. Her behavior was as free as her own home, even entering the Gilmore couple's bedroom. He called her up.

"Mrs. Lynn! You may be friends with Mrs. Gilmore, but you must refrain from going into other people's bedrooms. Keeping each other's privacy is the morality of American society. Buddhism is the saying of a person's behavior and Buddhism is society. It's important to care about small things to win people's trust."

One day, they are all the ones who will be the backbone of the Great propagation of Buddhism in the U.S.A. That's why he thought that he needs to advise even behaviors which is like normal. It can be said as bringing up human resources by himself. Then Ishikawa, Director, came to his side and sat down.

"This worries me. They have no common sense and know nothing about things, including those appointed as leaders. I'm worried if they can do this well. We really don't have any talented person."

The tone was as looking down upon the comrade. Daisaku

Ikeda replied with great surprise.

"I never think so. They're all talented people. From now on, they will shine. All of them are pioneers in the history of Great propagation of Buddhism if they devote themselves to faith. I'm looking forward to the future."

Ishikawa said, "Ho!" and left the room.

It is certain that people who were appointed to the leaders lacked experience as managers and did not receive training. Also, social position or situation was not that excellent. However, the members encouraged each other in faith with hard works again and again in the foreign land of the U.S. They know the grief and distress of the people than anyone else. If that's the case, we must say that they are the most worthy people who have the noblest mission who will decorate the whole epic poetry, as to say Great propagation of Buddhism as leaders.

He could not help thinking that each and each person was a gemstone of a diamond that glittered in seven colors.

Nietzscheanism is completed by SGI this way

Part 11

Chairman Kosygin

Fall of 1973.

The Soviet Union has been trying to find out whether it is possible to visit the Soviet Union by Daisaku Ikeda, President of the Soka Gakkai International. President Ikeda immediately sent an answer.

"I will visit the Soviet Union if I can receive the opportunity to help promote cultural exchanges between the Soviet Union and Japan and build everlasting peace."

At that time, Kovalenko was in charge of Japan as vice president of the So-Il Association in the International Department of the Soviet Communist Party. He praised the Soka Gakkai International and insisted that the Soviet Union actively interact with the SGI. But most of the Communist Party officials of the Soviet Union were not fully aware of President Ikeda, who was leading the Soka Gakkai International and its organization.

They questioned whether Marxism-Leninism which denies religion and Soka Gakkai International which is a religious organization could understand each other, and even many people looked Ikeda suspiciously, who, to China, suggested the normalization of diplomatic relations with Japan, which is in tension with the Soviet Union. Under such circumstances, Kovalenko repeatedly insisted that Ikeda should be invited.

"We need to realize Ikeda's visit to the Soviet Union. We have to have a summit and welcome at the national level."

Kovalenko knew well who has the real power to bridge the rift and connect between China and Japan. Of course, he firmly believed President Ikeda should be invited to the Soviet Union.

Kovalenko strongly insisted whether the Soka Gakkai International, which has nearly 10 million members, will become friendly or anti-Soviet is an extremely important issue. Eventually, the Communist Party's political bureau, especially Chairman Kosygin, agreed to his passionate assertion.

The Soviet Union began to carefully consider how to invite President Ikeda. Daisaku Ikeda is the president of the Soka

Gakkai International and religious person. The Soviet Union is a communist country. Problems arise when the party invites him. So the Soviet Union took the form of Moscow University's invitation to President Ikeda, the founder of Soka University.

Ikeda's preparations for a visit to the Soviet Union were made steadily. But few were in favor of his visit to the Soviet Union. In other words, even the leaders of the SGI opposed the idea including even Vice President Joo-jo.

In a temple in Tokyo, it is said that the temple's head priest spoke to a leader of the women division of the SGI.

"Why Mr. Ikeda goes to a country that has no believers and denies religion."

They could not understand Ikeda's heart because they failed to realize the Buddhist's mission, 'realizing world peace'. Another important person of the financial world also said like this.

"Communist countries are becoming increasingly stagnant. It's never going to be good to be close to them. It's better to stop visiting the Soviet Union. By the way, why do you want to go to a place like the Soviet Union?"

Ikeda responded clearly, thanking the man for his concern.

"Because there are humans there. I'm going to meet humans. Isn't it the human heart that wants peace, whether it's a communist or a capitalist? So I go to put the bridge between the human' heart. I believe it is the surest way to realize peace!"

It was a determined tone of voice, fearing nothing. At his words, the person of the financial world nodded his head loudly with an admiring look.

"Did you think that far? I was impressed by that meaning. I wish you a successful visit to the Soviet Union."

the fall of 1974.

Moscow was a beautiful city. The trees on the street were being blown in a refreshing breeze, as the leaves, which had just begun to color, were like playing the melody of peace.

President Ikeda and his company arrived at a Russian hotel about 40 minutes from the airport. It was a modern hotel with even 3,000 rooms. Beyond the window of the room was the Kremlin surrounded by red brick walls, and the beautiful onion-shaped castle Basili temple, which is now a museum, was standing.

When Ikeda and his wife, Kaneko, after putting their luggage in order, they immediately began reciting the Sutra. Everything begins with the pray. This was their belief and their principle of action. The origin is an oath and determination. A small but a serious voice of reciting Sutra reverberated in the room.

It was a sincere prayer that one day, for the sake of the happiness and peace of the Soviet people, the Bodhisattva of Earth would be born on this land and do the active work. There is a holy saying: "If you move the Buddha, any trees and grass cannot unshaken, and any water cannot be confused.". The great saint Nichiren was convinced that a connection to the wonderful law, which is the fundamental of the whole, can change everything.

At 6:30 p.m. on that day, about 10 people from the Soviet Union, including the President of Moscow University, Hoffrop, attended the 'Friendship banquet' at the restaurant where President Ikeda and his company were staying. The president gave a welcome speech.

"Today is a day to celebrate of the Soviet Union we already know Ikeda's activities and instructions. The people of the Soviet Union have a deep understanding and sympathy for the activities of the Soka Gakkai International. I particularly appreciate the view of peace and the passion for education seen at Soka University."

Members of the SGI who accompanied Ikeda were surprised. They were shocked because President of Moscow University, who met him for the first time, marveled at his deep understanding of President Ikeda and the movement of the SGI and Soka University. But it was no wonder that the Soviet Union turned its eyes to the Soka Gakkai International and studied it.

The SGI, at after war(World War 2), started from almost nothing to the 3,000 members when Josei Toda was appointed as the second President in 1951. In just 20 years, however, it has become Japan's largest religious organization with '10 million members'. Furthermore, the unknown people became the main leader of social construction, pushing for reforms in various fields such as culture, education, and politics, creating a great trend for the people. Indeed, it was so wonderful that it can be said as the 'miracle of modern times'.

Meanwhile, it was a very natural trend for Soviet leaders, who were agonizing over how to bring about the vitality of the people in order to develop their motherland, to become deeply interested in the Soka Gakkai International and its President, Daisaku Ikeda.

Ikeda used every possible effort to build up an unprecedented

SGI's history, encouraging his fellows and striving for his struggle. But members of Soka Gakkai

who visited the Soviet Union with him seemed to think that his struggle and the great success of the SGI were natural. So they didn't notice why Hoffrop and others were paying attention to the Soka Gakkai International.

The president concluded his speech.

"I am very happy to have the opportunity to talk to Ikeda about education for the future of mankind in the 21st century. Then let's congratulate and cheers for this meeting!"

After the toast, Ikeda said hello.

"The Sokka Gakkai is Japan's largest organization created voluntarily by the Japanese people. Our concern is human peace and the well-being of the people. And I think education should be 'the fountain of eternity' that will create a peaceful and prosperous 21st century. In that sense, I'm very happy to visit your country and exchange education with you. And I'd be happier if I could shine the lanterns of friendship with people from various classes."

After saying so, he expressed his aspirations imagining the future.

"Just as people feel human warmth in the winter of beautiful

Siberia when they see the light escaping through the window, we also want to cherish the lamp of the human mind, although the social system may be different. Just as spring comes to the frozen land of Siberia and plants sprout, I believe that the future of mankind will surely bring a spring full of hope."

After the SGI President's greeting, everyone had a good time over dinner. There Ikeda made his point clear.

"I think building a bridge of friendship requires looking 100 or 200 years ahead and opening the way for the generations to follow. So I consider educational exchanges to be the most important. I believe that if Japan and the Soviet Union, and the world, are united eternally, it will create a tide of world peace."

Daisaku Ikeda's grand idea of education was born out of Buddhism's humanistic philosophy. Furthermore, he also mentioned the U.N. of education. The U.N. of education means that all universities and students should be allowed to transcend the walls of state or ideology, to make scrams and create world peace. President Hoffrop has been deeply concerned by the idea.

"What an interesting and important proposition!"

The people of the Soviet Union also mentioned their

Nietzscheanism is completed by SGI this way

education policies one after another. It was such a passionate conversation that the ice cream served as dessert melted away.

Ikeda said.

"Ice cream also melted by the warmth of friendship. This is the Soviet drink!"

The laughter spread. The last night of Moscow, which was filled with the joy of friendship, grew deeper and deeper, as his humor gradually mingled with the hearts of the people around him. As the banquet was in the climax. Kovalenko, vice president of the So-Il Association, approached Ikeda and whispered:

"Mr. Ikeda! The good news is waiting for you. Chairman Kosygin wants to see you at 10 a.m. tomorrow."

Ikeda also thought he would have a meeting with Chairman Kosygin if possible. Because there were a lot of things he wanted to talk to the Chairman in person to open the way for world peace. In particular, he thought the need for talking about the Chinese leader's desire for peace.

He said, "Okay. I'll visit you as a courtesy visit."

The next day, at 10 a.m.

As Ikeda entered the conference room, Chairman Kosygin

was seen. Keen eyes, wrinkles on the forehead, and a tightly sealed mouth. The Chairman's face showed a strong will in charge of the Soviet Union's heavy responsibilities, the leader of the eastern camp, with Secretary Brezhnev. The Chairman is seventy years old. However, he was full of vitality.

Ikeda smiled and approached Kosygin and asked for a handshake.

"Thank you for taking the time even though you are busy. It's an honor to meet you!"

The Chairman also said with a smile on his face.

"I've been looking forward to seeing Ikeda, too!"

After greeting, Ikeda and Kosygin entered the conference room and sat face to face with the long table between them. To the right of the Chairman sat Kovalenko, vice chairman of the So-Il Association, and to the left sat the principal instructor of Moscow University, who translated. People like photographers from the 「Seikyo Newspaper」 who accompanied President Ikeda had to be outside.

President Ikeda asked the Chairman in a posture like moving himself forward.

"Can I give my opinion straight?"

The Chairman nodded.

Nietzscheanism is completed by SGI this way

"I learned more about your country during this visit. I also know that your country is trying hard to ease tension in the world. But that attitude was unfortunately not passed on to Japan. To be honest with you, the Japanese are familiar with Russian literature and Russian folk songs, but they do not feel friendly to the Soviet Union. It's because they have the impression that Russia is a 'country of fear' somehow.

If you really want to tell the truth and gain the understanding of the Japanese, you should not only have limited exchanges with pro-Soviet politicians but also have extensive exchanges. You should meet more aggressively with people who don't like the Soviet Union or with Conservative Members. Also, politics and economics alone can't really make friendships. Cultural exchange is the most important thing."

President Ikeda talked just as his thinking even if it might be rude to Chairman Kosygin. Kosygin nodded widely as Ikeda finished speaking.

"I agree! I will review what I will do in the future based on Ikeda's opinion."

President Ikeda felt the size of generosity because of Chairman Kosygin's sincere manner. He thought 'he speaks the same language!'.

Chairman Kosygin is famous for not showing his emotion on his face. At the young age of 34, he started his career as a member of Cabinet, and after then he was appointed as the important positions of the government and party. But one day he had said this to a close friend of his.

"In the days of Stalin, we could never be alone, because we were being watched by the Party. If somebody did wrong deeds, or even without wrong deeds, he/she will be subject to a purge, simply. It was a miracle and luck to have survived so far."

Chairman Koshin told President Ikeda over a long period of time, including his thoughts on the peace treaty of the Soviet Union. Ikeda said as Chairman closed the story.

"We hope that we continue to discuss the issue with the foreign minister and other government officials. Our Soka Gakkai International is an organization of Buddhists, so it stands up in religious beliefs and aims for world peace."

Ikeda wanted Chairman to recognize that the SGI and the Komeito party were in different situations and that religious group and political party were different. So he felt that the courage to speak clearly is needed. "Many of the misfortunes in this world have been caused by misunderstanding and lack of explanation, not having enough words is hindering work,"

Dostoevsky, a Russian literary giant once said.

President Ikeda continued to speak.

"I have created a Komeito party, but between the SGI and the Komeito party, we separate the finance and personnel and operate them independently. So I don't get involved in party affairs and leave political issues to the Komeito party."

He then mentioned the history of the Soka Gakkai International and said the SGI struggled against the suppression of the military government. Mr. Koshin quietly accepted, asking Ikeda:

"You, President has founded and established the Komeito party as a Buddhist, and what is your fundamental ideology?"

Ikeda answered right away.

"It is pacifism, culturalism, and educationism. The fundamentals of that are humanism."

The Chairman's eyes glowed at the words of translation. And admiringly smiled contently. Speaking in a lively, loud voice, Chairman Kosygin, who heard what a fundamental ideology was from the president of the Soka Gakkai International.

"I appreciate the idea that Ikeda has. I think that we should realize that idea as well. Now, the President said, "pacifism," but our Soviet Union values peace and our first rule is not starting a war."

The conversation moved on to the subject that President Ikeda most wanted to talk about. Ikeda said with a flush on his cheek.

"That's a great idea. You must avoid war! I went to Leningrad and visited the cemetery. The tremendous sacrifices made by the Soviet Union during World War II have been deeply embedded in my life. I felt keen that both the people and the leaders of your country wanted peace together."

In Ikeda's heart came a strong rage against the war. He spoke of the impression of visiting the cemetery, thinking of the struggles of the Leningrad people surrounded by Nazi German and lost their lives in hunger and cold.

"The Soviet people had a very harsh experience. This should never happen again!"

At this time, the Chairman's eyes flashed. He looked quietly into Ikeda's eyes and listened to the following: Ikeda asked the Chairman.

"Where were you during World War II?"

The Chairman answered quietly. "I was in Leningrad when Leningrad was surrounded by Nazi German."

There was a pause after saying this. Mr. Koshin seemed to

Nietzscheanism is completed by SGI this way

recall that time. Such a history should never be repeated if one knew the misery of war. In the Chairman's eyes, the resolution of peace-building was burning.

President Ikeda said in a strong tone as he stared at Chairman Kosygin.

"Like the Soviet people, the Chinese people were eager for peace. China was by no means an aggressor state!"

The conversation grew more and more into the climax. President Ikeda told Chairman Kosygin how he actually felt when he visited China three months ago.

"The Chinese Chairman made it clear that China never attacks other countries first. But he was preparing for the attack by digging up an air-raid shelter, fearing that the Soviet Union would attack him. China is looking at the Soviet Union's attitude. I'll be honest with you. Will the Soviet Union attack China?"

The Chairman stared at Ikeda with keen eyes. The sweat stood on his forehead And said as if determined.

"No, the Soviets are not willing to attack China! I don't intend to isolate China for collective security is guaranteed in Asia."

"Is that so? Can I deliver the message to China as it is?"

Chairman Kosygin was silent for a moment. Then in a determined tone, he spoke to President Ikeda in a firm tone.

"You can tell them that the Soviet Union will not attack China!"

Ikeda looked at the Chairman with a smile.

"Then wouldn't it be good for the Soviet Union to get along with China?"

The Chairman had a puzzled look on his face for a moment but immediately smiled. Resonance of the mind and heart made a scene of laughter. Ikeda was certainly rewarding in the talks. The conversation was the sun that pierced the block and poured out the light of hope for the future.

The talks have already been over an hour and a half. The chairman's scheduled time must have passed. President Ikeda thought he shouldn't drag anymore.

"Thank you very much for your time, even though you are busy today."

The Chairman replied with a smile.

"I'm happy to have a meaningful conversation. The issue raised by you, President Ikeda, is very important. It's not just about politics and economics, but about many other areas."

After the meeting, President Ikeda presented the Japanese

Nietzscheanism is completed by SGI this way

picture. Chairman Kosygin gave the silver medal celebrating the Soviet Union's 50th anniversary. In their farewell, the Chairman held Ikeda's hand tightly and said,

"Please contact me when you come to Moscow. Let's see each other again!"

"Thank you, Chairman! I look forward to seeing you again."

When Ikeda came out from the interview room, his interpreter at Moscow University approached him with an excited look.

"I've been moved! It was a very fruitful meeting."

President Hoffrop, who was standing next to his principal instructor, held Ikeda's hand tightly.

"I was extremely happy listening to the contents of the talks. I think it was a 100-point conference that opened up a great flow of friendship between the Soviet Union and Japan."

Ikeda said.

"Thank you. I was able to have a heart-to-heart talk. I was deeply impressed by the heart and character of Chairman Kosygin, who loves peace!"

It is said that Kosygin, who came home late that night, said this to his beloved daughter, Guvishani.

"Today, your dad met a very interesting and excellent

Japanese man."

It was in late 1980 when President Ikeda heard about Chairman Kosygin's news of his death. It was right after Kosygin had just resigned in October of that year because of illness. Kosygin's life was a great life, complete with his mission to the last moment. All the citizens of the Soviet Union mourned his death.

Ikeda paid a visit to Kosygin's grave in May the following year. After the visit, he paid a courtesy visit to Mrs. Guvishani, the daughter of the dead, Kosygin. She gave a crystal vase and two books to President Ikeda in tears.

"All the family members agreed to give Ikeda father's belongings. This book contains the warmth of my father. I'll give it to you on my father's behalf."

The fine vase was a prize that the chairman was honored as a 'socialist labor hero', two books were his last work written by the chairman, and a family heirloom of the Kosygin's family that laid in his study until the moment of his death.

Time goes by and by. Either the Soviet Union or the world has changed dramatically. Soon, the confrontation between China and the Soviet Union was over and the Cold War ended. The Soviet Union has chosen the path of 'democracy'.

Nietzscheanism is completed by SGI this way

Ikeda was recalling meeting then Chairman Kosygin.

President asked Chairman Kosygin.

"Can I think the 21st century is bright?"

Then the prime minister replied.

"We sincerely hope so, too!"

The Chairman's powerful voice revived around the President's ear.

Part 12

Premier Zhou Enlai

It has been two months since President Ikeda returned from a visit to the Soviet Union. A letter of invitation delivered from Beijing University in China through the Chinese Embassy in Japan arrived at the headquarters of the Soka Gakkai International. It was mid-November 1974.

This was written on the invitation.

"We have no doubt that Ikeda's visit to China will strengthen the friendship between the two countries, as well as the friendship between Beijing University and Soka University. Please visit China!"

When President Ikeda first visited China, he once handed over 5,000 books, including Japanese books, to Beijing University as a donation list to build up cultural exchanges with

Nietzscheanism is completed by SGI this way

China. It was six months ago. Now that the book had arrived, they wanted to hold the ceremony.

President Ikeda was thinking that he should visit China as soon as possible and deliver Chairman Kosygin's words to the Chinese leadership. He also hoped to visit China once again to promote cultural exchanges with China. He graciously accepted the invitation of Beijing University.

Two weeks later, on the morning of December 2, Ikeda left Haneda Tokyo International Airport with his wife, Kaneko. The morning in Tokyo was cold bitingly. A bitter north wind blew in from Hokkaido and penetrated into the body.

Late in the afternoon of the same day, a company of President Ikeda arrived at Beijing Airport. The weather in Beijing, which had barely stopped snowing since morning, was cold, with temperatures dropping below freezing. When Ikeda stood in the trap, a cold wind blew up her cheeks.

'Go against the cold wind!' This was Ikeda's belief.

There were many people at the airport, including the representative of Beijing University. The head of the library, the student representative and the secretary of the Sun-Peace Sino-Japanese Friendship Association welcomed the chairman's party with a smile.

The following day, a welcoming ceremony was held under the auspices of Beijing University. The venue was the Beijing Hotel where Ikeda's party would stay.

The representative of Beijing University said.

"Mr. Ikeda visited our country last May, and even after returning home, he published a great deal of text. Through these writings, we were able to confirm Mr. Ikeda's sincere feelings towards the Chinese people!"

When Ikeda visited China for the first time, he continued to write a series of articles in newspapers and magazines to promote China's true face he experienced in China, not only to Japan but also to the world. He wrote unsleepingly. On the deep night of writing, his shoulders tightened, his throat hurt, and his arms didn't go up. But he wrote it in silence.

The strength of the pen is strong. True media casts out the true light of truth, driving out the false darkness and bringing the sun of courage to people's minds. The media's brave man is as a million troops.

China's leadership praised President Ikeda's hard work while keeping a close watch on the media activities. In particular, Premier Zhou Enlai was paying keen attention to the activities of the Soka Gakkai International and young President's activity.

Nietzscheanism is completed by SGI this way

In reply to the welcoming speech, Ikeda said:

"I'm doing my best with the belief that education is my last business. Because 'human education' is the most important thing in promoting peace and culture. It is because I firmly believe that the building of ever-lasting world peace, the cooperation of races, the equality between nations, the society in which human beings can live as human beings are based on the foundation of 'education', and that education is 'the fountain of human culture' that provides society with new vitality that can always be extraordinary.

The Soka University, which I founded, features three categories: 'Be the Best of Human Education!', 'Be the Cradle of Building a New Culture!' and 'Be the Fortress of Peace of Mankind!' These mottos contained my expectation and hope that 'The younger generation will always stand by the people and pioneer a new future. They will protect the people, keep peace and contribute to the peaceful world!'.

I think this spirit will work at Beijing University as well. We hope that under the common goal of 'peace,' youth from both China and Japan will continue to develop in friendship from generation to generation through educational exchanges that open up the future together!"

Nietzsche and Ikeda

Peace is a secret garden of mankind. It must be the most important mission of the highest academic department to realize that. No matter how good a university is, the education has already failed if it only produces a ruthless elite who is indifferent to the suffering of agonies such as war, hunger, poverty, and discrimination. Thus, human education forms the basis of all.

Make a human!

Grind the heart of benevolence and justice!

There's a starting point where education has to go back!

The people at the reception were in full bloom with a joyful discourse on peace education and educational exchanges. Everyone was bright and joyful.

A good book is always a nutritious element of spirit for young people and is a great teacher who understands different cultures and knows the harmonious human world.

Tolstoy said.

"Reading a good book inspires a desire for good!"

The reception led to a meeting. Ikeda spoke with Zhao Fu-chu, vice-chairman of the Chinese Buddhist Association at the same table, on the topic of Lotus Sutra. During Ikeda's first visit to China, the two briefly talked in the subject of Lotus Sutra. Then, it was a place to talk about an unfinished conversation.

The conversation began with how to pronounce 'That moment Sakya' which is the second beginning of the Skillful Means(方便品). Ikeda pronounced it in Japanese and had the interpreter read it in Chinese.

"Ershishizun(爾時世尊)"

Zhao Fu-chu then immediately went on to say "Congsanmei (從三昧)" in Chinese. He apparently realized the depth of the Buddhist scriptures and memorized the scriptures.

The two men's conversations reached the meaning of the 'Text(本文)', 'Theoretical Teaching(迹門)', 'Skillful Means(方便品)', 'Life-span(壽量品)', and even 'Ten worlds(十界)'.

Ikeda said.

"Lotus Sutra is the law explaining human life. My teacher Josei Toda who was arrested because of the oppression of the military government decided to read the whole contents of Lotus Sutra and repeated the Reciting the holy phrase and thinking. After all, he realized 'Buddha exactly means life'. Today the reason for Soka Gakkai International being developed this much is the realization of the teacher"

Zhao Fu-chu was listening to Ikeda with interest. He said with a twinkle in his eyes as Ikeda ends his words.

Nietzsche and Ikeda

"I think his student, Ikeda, has developed Buddhism greatly in modern style, the SGI can be developed. When I hear the words of Mr. Ikeda, "Ah! I can understand the Buddhism this way!'. I feel like my eyes are wide open. It cannot be the living teaching with just understanding old scriptures, but spreading the whole new teaching."

Ikeda replied Zhao Fu-chu.

"It's very important to have new teaching. I'd like to spread the teaching of the essence of Lotus Sutra which was systemized in your country, China(By Editor: It means the Buddhist scripture of three thousand realms in a single moment of life written by monk T'ien-ta'i of China), to the world."

"Please do so, Please!"

Zhao Fu-chu said so and looked at Daisaku Ikeda with a respectful glance.

Conversation is like a wave that is coming and going. Just as waves one day change the shape of a rock, so if you open your heart and talk faithfully, distrust can be turned into faith. Daisaku Ikeda's visit to China was a very journey of dialogue.

The next morning.

At the Beijing Hotel, Ikeda spoke with several people

including Zhang Xiangshan, vice chairman of the Sino-Japanese Friendship Association. In terms of how to maintain human peace forever, exchanging views on various issues between China and Japan, Sino-Soviet Union relationship, moreover, Asian and global issues.

Ikeda said with his thoughts.

"China should take the path of peace and friendship with the Soviet Union as well as the United States!"

Then the Chinese side expressed their views on all the situations both inside and outside, stressing that although difficulties may follow, they also intend to move on to the 'road of peace'.

As Italian poet Petrarca said, "Look, how time flies so fast! How fast life goes by!", time flies by in a flash.

Daisaku Ikeda spoke clearly of his resolution and the topic to be addressed.

"As a civilian, I will further promote exchanges between the people in the sense of creating a base stream to world peace. In particular, I will visit countries that have long been plagued by aggression and oppression to build a bridge of peace and friendship. We must not repeat confrontation, hostility, and war forever! I'd like to change it!"

Two and a half hours passed in the blink of an eye.

Times move. Times change. To do so, we must first move the human mind. When a person changes, history certainly changes.

December 5, 1974.

It was the last day of the stay. Daisaku Ikeda and his wife Kaneko held a return banquet at an international club in downtown Beijing. The Sino-Japanese Friendship Association, officials from Beijing University, press officials and employees of the Beijing Hotel who were indebted during their stay also invited.

It was about the end of the banquet. Liao Chung-zu, President of the Sino-Japanese Friendship Association, was absent because of the call. Maybe it was a phone call. When Liao returned to his seat, he let Ikeda know something in a small voice.

"Mr. Ikeda! Actually, Premier Zhou is waiting."

It was a sudden notification. In a meeting with Deputy Prime Minister Deng Xiaoping, Ikeda politely declined the speech, saying that Zhou's illness was heavier than he had expected.

"No! I can't meet Premier Zhou. The meeting is detrimental to Premier's health. I'll only accept that mind in gratitude."

Nietzscheanism is completed by SGI this way

Then Liao said, with a very embarrassed look on his face.

"Premier Zhou strongly hopes for a meeting. The Premier seems determined to meet with you, President Ikeda no matter what!"

It seems that it is no longer a situation to refuse. Ikeda said.

"All right, I'll meet him! But I'll meet him only for a moment and come out right away. It is because I don't want to harm the health of the Prime Minister."

In fact, at this time, Premier Zhou's health was never in a situation in which he could make interviews or anything. Premier Zhou's medical staff also opposed the meeting.

"If you enforce the meeting, Your life cannot be guaranteed, Premier!"

However, Premier Zhou said with fortitude.

"I must see President Ikeda no matter what!"

It was obvious that he was desperate. His words made the medical staff embarrassed. The medical staff was forced to talk to the prime minister's wife, Mrs. Deng Ying-chiao, and ask her to persuade him. But she respected Premier Zhou's will.

"If Comrade En says so, please grant the meeting."

His wife must have felt the Premier's deep feelings for Ikeda.

Before leaving the hotel, Ikeda told Liao Cheng-zu.

"I'll only go in with my wife. If he talks to several people, the Prime Minister could be tired."

Daisaku Ikeda thought doing so was the least amount of consideration they could. He went out. The air outside was biting cold. The temperature seemed to be below zero.

The party split up into cars and drove along the dark road at a rapid pace. By about 15 minutes, the car arrived at the front door of a building. It was a 305 hospital where Premier Zhou was hospitalized. As the group stepped down from the car and entered the building, Premier Zhou, who had changed his cloth into a people's suit, stood there waiting for President Ikeda's party.

When Ikeda put out his right hand, Premier Zhou held his hand firmly with a smile.

"Good to see you!"

Ikeda's left hand helped as supporting the right arm. In 1939, during Revolutionary Struggle, the prime minister fell off his horse and suffered a broken upper right elbow. He knew that the aftereffect had bent his right arm.

The Prime Minister's hands are white. It was similar to the hands of a teacher, Toda who was weak in later life. Ikeda was heartbroken. The two looked directly at each other. Ikeda felt

Nietzscheanism is completed by SGI this way

admirable and excellent spirit form the entire body of Premier which was lean.

Premier Zhou spoke softly.

"Let's all take a photo together first!"

The Premier shook hands as he spoke to all the members who accompanied him. Since it was a meeting with the Premier, everyone took a photo of him with a nervous face. When the shooting was over, Premier Zhou told President Ikeda.

"Come on, this way!"

As the two sides discussed earlier, only Ikeda and Kaneko entered the conference room. When everyone sat down, Premier Zhou spoke in a quiet tone to Ikeda.

"This is your second visit to China, isn't it? Last time you came, I couldn't see you because of my poor health. But I also wanted to meet you because my health is getting better little by little. I'm very happy to see you this time!"

Premier Zhou was seventy-six and Ikeda was forty-six. Maybe the Premier may be counting on the possibility of Ikeda's youth.

"To accomplish great things, you must be young."

This is Goethe's proverb. A new force is shaping the future. Therefore, we should devote our energy to nurturing the younger generation.

Lin Li-win, director of the Sino-Japanese Friendship Association, translated. Ikeda's wife, Kaneko, eagerly recorded the conversations between the two, thinking 'This must be an important historical interview!'.

Zhou praised Ikeda's efforts to enhance exchanging friendly relations between China and Japan.

"Mr. Ikeda has appealed to us that no matter what happens, we should develop the friendly relations among people of China and Japan. I'm very happy. Sino-Japanese friendship is a common wish for us. Let's try together!"

Though speaking quietly, the Premier's voice contained power. President Ikeda felt in his words that the Premier's spirit of opening the eternal path of Sino-Japanese friendship was crying out. He also felt like receiving the baton of peace.

Premier Zhou glowed his eyes and said as if he were determined.

"Did you talk with Deputy Prime Minister Deng Xiaoping yesterday? Mr. Ikeda's reputation is well known by officials, including the deputy prime minister. I don't have to go into details about that, should I?"

The contents of the Soviet Union seemed to have reached the

Nietzscheanism is completed by SGI this way

ears of Premier Zhou.

"Yes, it is. Well, we'll excuse ourselves because it is bad for your health."

The Premier then shook his head slowly as if he wanted them to stay. Then he asked their hometown. Ikeda replied.

"Both of us are from Tokyo. The character of the Tokyo native is cool and simple. but, not smart. We can only play one person's part, even we are two."

Ikeda replied with humor. he wanted to soften the Premier's heart a bit. Consideration is the starting point of sincerity. The Premier laughed cheerfully. It was the first time he heard his laugh. Then the Premier squinted at the other side and said as he is missing it.

"I left Japan more than 50 years ago when the cherry blossoms were blooming!"

Ikeda said, nodding his head.

"Yes! Please visit Japan again at the time of the cherry blossoms."

But the Premier smiled in a lonesome way.

"I hope so, but I don't think it will be possible."

Ikeda's heart ached. Then a note was handed over to the interpreter, Lin Li-wen. It said, "Premier! You must rest now." It was a memo from a medical team.

Lin Li-yun, who is in charge of translation, handed a memo to Premier. But Premier kept saying without even looking at the memo as if he knew it all. Even if his life span was shortened, he had a stronger mind that he needs to meet Ikeda and say what he wanted to say at any cost.

Ikeda refrained from making aggressive comments, thinking that he should not tire Premier. He gave several glances to Liao Cheng-zu, chairman of the Sino-Japanese Friendship Association, who was present with him, saying, "It would be better to finish the meeting."

But each time, Liao sent a signal saying, "It's still okay."

Ikeda said with his heart.

"Premier Zhou should always be healthy. China stands at the center of world peace. You have to live long for your country and for the 800 million people."

Then the Premier said with all his might.

"Mr. Ikeda said China is at the center of the world, but we will not be a superpower country. Also, China is not yet financially sufficient. But I will contribute to the world. I think this 25 years of the 20th century will be the most important time in the world of mankind. People all over the world have to

Nietzscheanism is completed by SGI this way

help each other in an equal position."

Ikeda wrote Premier's words in his mind as if he were listening to a will.

The interview lasted about half an hour. President Ikeda wanted to talk to Premier Zhou longer. But he thought he shouldn't take any more time.

Saying "I'll certainly say your will to the place where it is needed. Thank you very much for meeting me!", he finished the meeting.

In commemoration of his visit, President Ikeda gave Japanese paint 'The lespedeza and wagon'. After the Ikeda party left, the prime minister lowered the picture hanging on the wall and changed it into one given by Ikeda.

There is a saying in the Chinese classics: "When two people share their minds, the sharpness cuts the iron." It means that strong friendship can cut even the hardest metal.

This was Premier Zhou and Chairman Ikeda's first and last time meeting in their lives.

On December 23, 1974, 18 days after his meeting with Ikeda, Premier Zhou headed for Changsa, Hunan Province, where Chairman Mao was located. This was to win an understanding to give Deng Xiaoping greater authority. For the sick Premier Zhou, this long trip risking his life.

The steward had to support the Premier when he boarded the airplane. His legs groaned and his hands trembled. It was difficult for him to peel the candy on board. However, he was desperate to meet with President Mao to create a trend that would push Sirenbang(四人帮; four important people) for China's future.

Finally, Premier Zhou won President Mao's consent. And Deng Xiaoping will be appointed to key posts at the Fourth National People's Congress next month, including the First Prime Minister and Vice President of the Military Commission.

Deputy Prime Minister Deng Xiaoping took full responsibility and worked hard on behalf of Premier Zhou, whose body was not free. It was when the surgery was operated four months before the prime minister passed away in September 1975. Premier asked, "Did Comrade Deng Xiaoping come?".

Vice Premier Deng hurried to his side, the prime minister threw his eyes at him and managed to reach out and hold Deng

Nietzscheanism is completed by SGI this way

Xiaoping's hand. The Prime Minister said barely.

"You've done a good job over the past year. You're stronger than I am."

Deng Xiaoping was moved.

"Nobleman dies for those who know him."

It's a famous phrase in 『The Memoirs of Han China』.

In January 1976, Premier Zhou Enlai passed away. Then four important people attacked Deng Xiaoping, and he fell to the ground again. However, when Mao passed away in September of that year, the four important people were arrested immediately the following month.

In July 1977, Deng Xiaoping returned to the Party and the government's posts and played as vice-president and deputy prime minister. Justice, too, becomes evil if it is defeated. Sad as it is, that is the reality of society. That is the trend of history. Therefore, he who goes the right way must never lose.

In August 1978, the foreign ministers of both China and Japan finally signed the Sino-Japanese Peace Treaty in Beijing. And in October, Deputy Prime Minister Deng Xiaoping and Foreign Minister Huang Hua visited Japan together to hold an exchange ceremony for the ratification.

Nietzsche and Ikeda

Part 13

Sato, former Prime Minister

Former Japanese Prime Minister Eisaku Sato won the Nobel Peace Prize.

He contacted the headquarters of the Soka Gakkai International saying he wanted to show it to President Kieda. It was December at the end of 1974. However, Daisaku Ikeda had a difficult schedule as he soon leaves for the U.S. on January 6, the following year.

After hearing about that, Sato said, "Then, we'll visit President Ikeda's house." President Ikeda thought that 'I'm sorry to take them to a small house.' and decided to hold a meeting at a Japanese restaurant near his house.

Ikeda doesn't live in a great house and lives in a modest one so far because he accepted the advice of his former mentor, the second President, Josei Toda who said to young Ikeda like this.

"We should not be too shabby as chairman of the Soka Gakkai International. But it's not good to live in a big mansion."

Daisaku Ikeda greeted the Sato couple with his wife, Kaneko. Former Prime Minister Sato wore a suit and a green tie, and his hair looked a bit long. So, he looked younger.

Ikeda first congratulated him.

"I sincerely congratulate you on winning the Nobel Peace Prize."

Then, former Prime Minister Sato said shamefully.

"Thank you. I just wanted to show it to you, President Ikeda."

The two couples continued their conversation when taking meals. Former Prime Minister Sato said.

"On my way back from the Nobel Prize ceremony, I visited the Soviet Union and met Chairman Kosygin. We didn't discuss territorial issues between the two of us, but we had a friendly conversation for about an hour. Actually, Kosygin said, 'Please send my regards to President Ikeda when you return to Japan. Recently, the two of us had a very meaningful and informative conversation.'"

Daisaku Ikeda nodded and said,

"Is it true! When I visited the Soviet Union in September last year, I met with Chairman Kosygin and told him my opinion frankly."

President Ikeda told former Prime Minister Sato in detail what happened during the meeting. Many Japanese people have the impression that 'The Soviet Union is a scary country', so they should change it, and that if they want to gain understanding from Japanese people, they should not only interact with politicians and organizations known as pro-Soviet groups but also with members of Assembly of a conservative party.

Former Prime Minister Sato is a well-known pro-American leader. Chairman Kosygin interviewed him, who was like that. Mr. Koshin seemed to take Ikeda's opinion seriously.

Courageous dialogue widens the waves of resonance and becomes the power to move the world. Sato listened to Ikeda and said, nodding his head widely.

"You moved Chairman Kosygin and made it possible meeting with me and him."

Ikeda replied.

"No, it was because Chairman Kosygin sincerely accepted my opinion. I think there is a greatness of Chairman Kosygin in that sincerity."

Nietzscheanism is completed by SGI this way

The thinker Uchimura Ganjo said,

"There has never been a man in the world who has not been sincere and who has become great." This was what Ikeda often said to his fellow juniors.

Sato said.

Even so, you, President Ikeda spoke very well to Chairman Kosygin. I think it's just advice from a friend. It would be difficult for a representative of the Government to have such a conversation. That's why private exchange is more important."

Sato learned from the trip but was impressed to learn that the University of Moscow had deep trust in President Ikeda and Soka Gakkai and Moscow had educational exchanges with each other as part of its extension.

In December last year, President Ikeda spoke with Premier Zhou Enlai and Vice-Premier Deng Xiaoping during his second visit to China and expressed his opinion that he wanted to cherish China. Then Sato said emphatically:

"Thank you for the bridge between China and Japan. You did a good job."

Former Prime Minister Sato is said to be close to Taiwan. However, Sato has long wanted to normalize diplomatic relations between China and Japan. Ikeda was well aware of the feeling.

Nietzsche and Ikeda

The reason why Sato has always valued Taiwan is that he has kept his faith in President Chiang Kai-shek. After the war, Sato felt a deep sense of grace for Chiang's quick recognition of the Japanese returning home and no war compensation.

Sato adhered to the belief that grace would be repaid by grace.

President Ikeda had a few chances to face Sato when he was prime minister. The deepest memory was nine years ago in January 1966, when he visited the Prime Minister's villa at Hatse of Kamakura.

In the villa, Ikeda talked alone with Sato for three and a half hours. Japan's future education, religion, international affairs and so on. It was a year and two months after Sato took office as Prime Minister. Sato was sixty-four years old, Ikeda was thirty-eight years old, and even their age gap was like a father and a son, but the two of them went beyond generations to have a heart-to-heart conversation with each other.

It was not long after the first volume of the novel 「The Human Revolution」 written by President Ikeda was published.

"I read 「The Human Revolution」. It's dignified and full of correct words. It can be said that one of the common people is greater than the prime minister."

Nietzscheanism is completed by SGI this way

Their conversation began with the novel, 『The Human Revolution』.

In the first volume of 『The Human Revolution』, Tsunesaburo Makiguchi, the first President of the Soka Gakkai said, "The reason I lament is not that a single sect is destroyed. It is because you know a country will be in destruction in front of your eyes obviously." It was an outrage against the Nichiren sect, which gave up its faith as a religious person submitting to the military government.

Sato spoke in a calm tone.

"The Soka Gakkai is pure. Hearts are clean. There are pure ideas for the country."

Ikeda and Sato had a little chat in the drawing room before moving to the dining table. They continued their conversation tasting the dishes served by Mrs. Sato. At that time, the Soka Gakkai and the Komeito Party were still not separated systemically. Sato, as the Prime Minister, may have intended to seek some cooperation from the party.

But no such story came up at all. Sato, looking forward to Japan's future, said his thoughts, sometimes deploring the Japanese attitude and mindset of life.

"The younger generation lost their minds thinking about the

future of the country. What a pity!"

Ikeda agreed. Sato went on the saying.

"It is very unfortunate that there is no young man who is trying to stand up for the future of mankind and the world. That's why I think the Soka Gakkai, which raises great young people, has a great mission."

Sato was also deeply concerned about the loss of ethics in Japan after the defeat.

"I am worried that there are religious ethics in Europe and the United States, while the Japanese have no ethics to control themselves. Furthermore, politicians who have to set an example for ethics are not at all exemplary. What a pity."

One of the great roles that religion should play is to establish ethics in people's minds. Sato seemed to be taking the subject of how to transform the human spirit.

When he finished eating, Sato led Ikeda into his room. As they walked up the stairs together, there was a picture hanging on the wall. The photo was taken by Yoshida Shigeru and Sato, who is famous for promoting Japan's reconstruction after the war.

"He is my teacher!"

Sato stretched out his chest and said proudly. When Ikeda saw the Prime Minister of a country proudly introducing his

Nietzscheanism is completed by SGI this way

teacher, he thought, 'What a reliable person'.

'The seeker of truth', and 'the improver' always admire the teacher. And he who has a teacher in his heart has a noble dignity.

Seneca, a Roman philosopher, said about his gracious teacher.

"If I do not respect him with the most grateful and dear heart, I am ungrateful."

Sato was called as an honor student at Yoshida School. It is said that he served Yoshida with sincerity as if he were treating strict father. He also acted with Yoshida during the 1955 conservative group joint action. He refused to join the New Party and the Liberal Democratic Party, which were major forces and spent some time as an independent member in a situation of isolation. He adhered to his teacher's faith.

Sato said to Ikeda.

"Your teacher is Mr. Toda, isn't he?"

"Yes, Josei Toda is my gracious teacher. Mr. Toda was a great mathematician, educator, and businessman. I got private tutoring from Toda and learned all kinds of study. I think I've got the best human education."

Ikeda replied proudly. Sato nodded with satisfaction. The

story continued in Sato's room.

"Mr. Toda is a great man. The power of the academic community, the power of the organization, is incredible. We have to follow the example of it."

The disciple is most pleased when his teacher is given a compliment. It's been a long time since Ikeda decided that it was his mission to do so.

In the Philippines, Sato Aisaku heard a report of his teacher, Yoshida Shigeru's death. He prepared national funeral contacting with Japan immediately with crying over and over as being devastated. After the war, there was no precedent for a national funeral in Japan. There were opinions against it. But he pushed hard because he wanted to show his teacher the highest honor.

Sato, who returned from a variety of overseas visits, rushed straight to Yoshida's home in Oiso Kanagawa, where his late teacher awaited him from Haneda Airport. The student's back, touching the face of his cold teacher, trembled. What did the student swear to his teacher?

Sato visited the United States the following month. Then he made the atmosphere of getting Ogasawara and Okinawa back. Actually, it was also a Yoshida's hidden wish.

It is a disciple to achieve his mentor's wishes. The student

Nietzscheanism is completed by SGI this way

must accomplish all the things that his teacher hoped for. That is 'the path of mentor and disciple' like the gold.

Sato served seven years and eight months in succession as Prime Minister for the longest time in history. During his tenure, he made contributions to signing the return of Okinawa, the ILO (International Labor Organization) treaty, and the Korea-Japan Basic Treaty.

It has already been nine years since the two people talked in Kamakura. As if to fill the void, Sato spoke of the future of Japan and the world with a bright smile.

Daisaku Ikeda listened to every word of Sato as if carving each and every word in life. It was because he felt the urge asking for the future from his words. Ikeda and Kaneko saw off returning Sato couple in their car.

Later, a polite letter from Hiroko Sato arrived at Ikeda's house. The letter said, "My husband's usually quiet, but he really talked a lot that day. 'I'm glad that the President has grown up more and works hard for Japan.' it said.

Sato collapsed three months after talking to Ikeda. And he ended up being a man who never came back.

Nietzsche and Ikeda

Part 14

Peru cultural festival

In March 1974, stars were shining brilliantly in the sky, and the airplane was flying towards Peru, South America. Maybe the airplane won't arrive in Lima until midnight.

President Daisaku Ikeda recalled March, eight years ago (1966) when he visited Lima, Peru, following Brazil. Then Lima was scheduled to meet him and hold a general meeting. However, in Peru at that time, Ikeda was suspected that the purpose of his visit was to prepare for a political party.

A Peruvian police official told a member of the group, "If we see anything inflammatory in this visit, we have no choice but to strengthen our wariness against the Peruvian Soka Gakkai International." There was a danger that Ikeda's presence at the general meeting might be seen as an 'incitement'.

Nietzscheanism is completed by SGI this way

Ikeda thought over and over. 'The members may be sad. But what matters is how to protect our members.' So he was forced to make a decision to cancel his participation in the general meeting.

More than 1,700 members were gathered from all parts of Peru at the general meeting. Some people came to the event by bus for several days. But there was no figure of Ikeda.

Eight years have passed since then.

After exiting the airplane trap, Chairman Kishibe greeted President Ikeda with a smile on his face. He had already turned sixty and had gray hair in sight, but habitually he had the same toughness as an old warrior. That Kishibe wept over his glasses and said, "Sensei, welcome!" and he could no longer speak.

"Congratulations! Peru won a great victory. You've worked really hard. I'll be indebted to you."

Saying this, Ikeda hugged Kishibe. Then a voice rang out from the airport building.

"Sensei! Sensei!"

When Ikeda turned his head and looked up, about 100 people were waving their hands from the rooftop of the airport building. Kishibe said apologetically.

"I firmly warned them not to come to the airport because it's too late, but they've come running to greet you somehow."

The next afternoon, the company of President Ikeda went out to look around the city. They wanted to see how the capital city of Lima looked and how people lived. The party visited Miraflores, a commercial center with many modern buildings along the coast.

The word Miraflores means 'beautiful street with flowers'. Like its name, various flowers were being blown by the wind in the park and in the avenue.

Ikeda found a tailor shop and went into the store. Kishibe asked following him.

"Do you want to buy a suit, Sensei?"

"Yes, I'd like to present you with some clothes."

President Ikeda felt a constriction in the chest by watching Kishibe in his old suit and his front teeth missing and welcoming him at the airport. He heard that Kishibe runs a stationery store besides a photo studio, but it seems that his life was not that prosperous. Perhaps he lived frugally, saving his living expenses, and traveled to the provinces for the members paying transportation.

It is an act of precious Bodhisattva to willingly pay his/

Nietzscheanism is completed by SGI this way

her own money for the Great propagation of Buddhism. The 'meaning' of that faith will be led to the eternal great luck and fortune.

Ikeda said with a smile.

"Mr. Kishibe has dedicated everything to the happiness of Comrade of Peru on my behalf. I'd like to give you a suit in return for your service. Well, choose what you like."

"No, that's..."

Kishibe was overwhelmed with gratitude and apologies.

"I didn't satisfy your expectations yet. It's just pathetic. I don't deserve to wear the clothes you buy me."

Ikeda spoke admonishingly.

"It's my little earnestness. Please think of it as a gift from your younger brother in Japan. Now, don't hesitate."

Then he began to choose clothes that would suit Kishibe.

"Sensei, that's too much...."

Kishibe cried, "I'm sorry. Then, I'll take your words without any hesitation," he said, with his head down deeply. There is gratitude to the humble. The heart of gratitude gives birth to emotion and impression and becomes a source of happiness. Kishibe chose a grey suit.

Nietzsche and Ikeda

The following day, at noon on the 25th, a company of President Ikeda visited Lima City Hall. Lima City was supposed to give President Ikeda the title of 'Special Honorary Citizen' so he would attend the ceremony.

The Lima City Hall was a magnificent building that made one feel a long history. The chandelier was shining brilliantly on the high ceiling. The welcoming speech of the intelligent mayor Arsamora, wearing glasses, echoed inside the room. Kimio Yoshino transferred his Spanish to Japanese.

"Peru is always looking for a new society with a lot of humanity with strong cohesion. In the meantime, we are very happy to have a large number of members of the Soka Gakkai International who are seeking to improve our humanity and practicing the dignity of life.

I think the reason why such a member can contribute to Lima City is possible because there is a leader like President Ikeda who aspire to world peace with practicing. Through the actions shown by the Soka Gakkai International, we were able to see the greatness of President Ikeda as a Buddhist, even a philosopher, historian, and thinker.

Today, our citizens of Lima are welcoming Mr. and Mrs. Ikeda. I am sure that this will make our Lima City and Soka

Nietzscheanism is completed by SGI this way

Gakkai International even more intimate. I would like to present Lima's key with the title of a Special Honorary Citizen."

Listening to the mayor Arsamora, Kishibe, Chairman of Peru, was desperate to swallow his tears. When Ikeda visited Peru eight years ago, everything seemed like a dream, considering that he was on the alert for government authorities and couldn't even attend a big ceremony.

Mayor Arsamora personally gave Ikeda a special citizenship certificate and the city key. There was loud applause. Kishibe continued to applaud, wetting his face with tears. The victory of a student was the victory of a teacher, and the victory of a teacher was the victory of a student. It is time for Ikeda to say hello.

"A little while ago, I received a certificate and the key of Lima from the mayor Arsamora, which means the best guest of Lima City. Thank you. This honor is something I will never forget."

Ikeda also thanked the whole city for their generous support for the Peru Cultural Festival. Kaneko, the President's wife, was also given the title of 'Honorary Citizen'. Then the mayor took the lead and guided the inside of the building himself. When he reached the place where the guest book was placed, the mayor

Nietzsche and Ikeda

asked President Ikeda to sign it. Ikeda wrote this.

"I became a citizen of Lima from today. I will work for Lima from today. I took responsibility for it from today. And I would like to wish Peru and Lima a better and better life, than anyone else."

A look of the mayor's company glowed as they watched the scene. Ikeda smiled for a joke at the pen.

"Now that I'm a citizen of Lima, I have to pay taxes."

The mayor replied to a humorous remark.

"I don't need any tax. However, please put your best efforts into the exchanges between Peru and Japan. That is the only wish of the people of Lima."

A laugh broke out. Humor is an expression of humanity that softens one's mind.

Eventually, the last day of the performance has come.

Everyone was waiting for the 'World Peace Peru Cultural Festival'.

Ikeda attended the cultural festival with many guests including Arsamora. The city theater where the performance would take place was a historic building representing Lima City. The festival started with the national anthem of Peru. The

Nietzscheanism is completed by SGI this way

stage was composed of two parts and fifteen acts.

Part I 'This Is My Peru' featured a variety of folk dances from different regions, including dances from the northern coast of Peru and dances with the joy of engaging in farming.

The total number of participants is about 900. They all danced in a cheerful and bright way as if to say, 'Look at this happy figure!' The background picture made by serial boards turned into a magnificent mountain, sea, and forest. At the back, dozens of male and senior members supported the boards with breathless pride. They were all filled with pride that they kept the cultural festival.

In the second part, the women's chorus began, followed by boy and girl dance, women's dance with the theme of friendship, and the performance of the music band and the drum and fife band, which were full of creative power for the future development. Among them, the most overwhelming power was the mass game of the four-story human pyramid of the men's division. Everyone stood up and applauded in that lively performance.

At last, 'the Peru Cultural Festival' was about to end.

At the finale, all the cast members of each program walked out onto the stage, shoulder-to-shoulder, and sang out the song

"Song of the New Century." It was the visit of President Ikeda, awaited and awaited for eight years. Tears of emotion were glistening in the eyes of all of them, who finally expressed, by the festival, the joy of winning praise and award in the fight against the misunderstanding and prejudice of society.

On the stage where the cast stood, President Ikeda, sitting in the box seats on the first floor, was clearly seen. There is also a Mayor in applaud in the next seat. Everyone in the cast cried out in their hearts as they reached the climax of the drama.

"Sensei! We did it. We won."

Only when the struggle is overcome can the song of winning be heard. The decorative flowers on the ceiling were divided, causing the colorful paper to a snowstorm and fluttering down in a splendid dance. It also poured down Ikeda's head.

He picked up a piece of paper that had fallen near his feet. The paper was cut into the shape of a cherry blossom petal. The hot feelings of all the members permeated his mind as he had heartbreaking feelings.

"Thank you." As he murmured, Ikeda picked petal and took it into an inside pocket gently as the precious mind of a friend was kept in mind. The move was being watched quietly by the Mayor Arsamora.

Nietzscheanism is completed by SGI this way

When the finale of joy ended, President Ikeda took the microphone in the box seat.

"What I want you to do is for each person to be an exemplary figure as a Peruvian citizen, and also to have a happy and peaceful life. And grow up as a Buddhist who can be praised by anyone, while making the utmost contribution to the community and building a new peace and prosperity in Peru."

Finally, he shouted.

"Viva, Peru! Viva, Lima!"

The cheers were shaking the old city theatre like turbulent waves.

Part 15

Doctor Peccei

SGI President Ikeda was scheduling a visit to Rome.

It was because the Vatican sent him a formal invitation to speak with the Pope in the Vatican.

Ikeda felt that it was very important to talk to Christianity in moving toward world peace. Talks with officials from the Roman Curia had already begun eight years ago.

Catholicism and Buddhism met and agreed that they wanted to build a foundation for understanding each other deeply and further achieving world peace. We believed that we could understand and cooperate with each other in terms of protecting human beings and building peace, although we had different doctrines. Also, Daisaku Ikeda extremely felt that without repeated dialogue with not only Christianity but also religions such as Islam, Judaism, and Hinduism, he could not create a big wave of world peace.

Finally, around the time of Ikeda's visit to Europe in 1975, a letter of invitation from the Roman Curia was sent. However, just before the departure, Nichiren Shoshu, one of monk organization of Nichiren Buddhism, began to show disapproval. Ikeda was very sorry, but his interview with the Pope was frustrated because he failed to get the final approval. If this meeting had been made, it would have been a very meaningful conversation for world peace. Unfortunately, however, the visit to Rome was canceled this way.

Ikeda asked Dr. Peccei in Rome to politely convey his apology to the Roman Curia. Then the doctor said,

"Then I'll go to Paris where the chairman is."

The Paris of May was covered with the fragrance of a new green. There were colorful flowers all over the street, as competing for each other's beauty.

As noon passed, Dr. Peccei, President of the Rome Club, arrived at the Paris Community Center of the Soka Gakkai International of France. The white-haired doctor stepped out of the car with a fresh look. Ikeda welcomed him with open arms.

"You've had a hard time coming the long way. Thank you very much. I came to Europe looking forward to meeting you, Mr. Peccei."

Ikeda led Dr. Peccei to the reception room of the Paris Community Center. The doctor showed the novel of Daisaku Ikeda, 『Human Revolution』 translated in English, and asked Ikeda for his autograph. Ikeda wrote like this.

"I, the author of 『Human Revolution』, sincerely wish and look forward to the success and performance of the Doctor who is the adviser and pioneer of the Humanity Revolution."

Meanwhile, Ikeda asked Dr. Peccei to sign the book about the conversation with Dr. Toynbee, 『A Conversation to Open the 21st Century』 was published in Japan. Dr. Peccei wrote like this.

"I deeply respect you, and I sincerely hope that all the pioneering work you do will bear fruit."

It was just the birthday of Dr. Peccei's wife. On such an important day, the doctor deliberately rushed from Italy to meet Ikeda. Ikeda was very sorry. The doctor was desperate to find a new breakthrough to save mankind that was on the brink of ruin. His keen eyes, with that desperate determination and strong responsibility, kept an eye on Ikeda.

As President Ikeda recalled the shout of the Josei Toda, who was the teacher of Ikeda, which was "Don't you people have the world's highest philosophy of philosophy of life?", he suggested to the doctor, "I'm sorry for the narrow room. Since the garden is beautiful, why don't we talk outside today?".

People living in the contemporary world need to know who Dr. Peccei is, who is the founder and President of the Rome Club, and what the organization, Rome Club is doing.

Dr. Peccei, who is also a prominent businessman, first held gathering in Rome, 1968 to appeal to the world's great scholars and managers to prevent the crisis of humanity. And they launched a private organization, the Roman Club.

The Roman club published a report about the crisis of mankind in 1972, 'the Limit of Growth' The report warned that if human life continues as it is, it will reach the limits of growth within 100 years due to food shortages, resource shortages, and environmental pollution, and eventually, mankind will face a state of destruction. The world was in shock.

Daisaku Ikeda, feeling the same sense of crisis, was very interested in the 'the Limit of Growth'. And he thought he'd meet with the Doctor and have a conversation. In line with the will of Ikeda, Eiji Kawasaki, the key man of the European Soka Gakkai International, had met with Dr. Peccei and told him about the ideology, purpose, and activities of the Soka Gakkai International.

A table and a sofa were set up in the garden, and a conversation began under the parasol. The doctor talked with enthusiasm.

"I have so far acted in the name of 'the Humanity Revolution'. And I thought, when digging it deeper, finally, the 'human revolution' can be reached. Please give me your opinion about the relationship between the two."

President Ikeda said, feeling sorry for his serious attitude.

"I think that the major premise of 'the Humanity Revolution' is the transformation of life forming humanity. The fundamental transformation of life is what we call 'the Human Revolution'. So for 'the humanity revolution', there must be 'the human revolution'."

And the doctor, who was listening to Ikeda silently, said, "Okay. I'll call it 'the Human Revolution' from today with a smile. And while mankind has so far experienced revolutions following advances in science and technology, such as the Industrial Revolution, the Doctor said that all these things are just 'the Revolution outside Human', whether the advanced technology is needed for happiness and prosperity of humans with emphasis.

Nietzscheanism is completed by SGI this way

"It's 'the Renaissance of the Human Mind'. It's a revolution of human by himself or herself. Mr. Ikeda has argued from before. That's what I paid attention to."

Cope with it while you still have time! This was the yelling of the doctor.

Dr. Peccei and President Ikeda talked on various topics. They talked over every problem, which mankind confronted, such as the need for cultural exchanges, the true figure of human education with a global perspective, how to grasp the situations of the times, and expectations for the U.N. and UNESCO, and also discussed the direction of the future sharply.

The doctor asked.

"How much time does it take for humans to make a human revolution? Human beings have a lot of difficult issues, such as nuclear weapons and environmental degradation. We can't wait 100 years for our own human transformation. We have to hurry."

President Ikeda answered.

"The movement to transform human beings should be gradual. It takes a lot of time. But if you don't act, if you don't sow, you won't be able to solve the situation. I just want to open a clue to the solution this century. I'm determined to sound the alarm for this matter by advising from various angles."

Appointed two and a half hours passed in the blink of an eye. Both of President Ikeda and Doctor Peccei had a lot to talk about still. Therefore, the two promised to exchange views through talks and letters continuously. For your information, they had five meetings after then and had many conversations through letters repeatedly.

At the last meeting of the two men in Paris, Dr. Peccei came running from the United States. It happened in June 1983. At that time the doctor had all his luggage stolen at the Paris airport. But to be punctual for the time of appointment, the Doctor drove a car even delaying the report of the robbery to the police.

In March 1984, the following year, the doctor passed away. He was seventy-five years old. The doctor was a man of great sincerity. He was a man who fought in frontline until his death to open the future of mankind. Just after that, the German version of the book about their talks had been published first. The title was 『Before it's too late』. And in October of that year, the Japanese version was published with the English version. The Japanese version is titled as 『Alarm for the 21st-century』.

The book was translated into 17 languages including Chinese and Spanish.

Today, mankind started to take environmental problems such as global warming caused by air pollution seriously. The pioneer who shouted it was the Doctor.

"It is the young man who can transform the world. The world changes with the human revolution of youth."

That was what the doctor said to his son in his later years.

Part 16

Konosuke Matsushita

Konosuke Matsushita started as a nine-year-old shopkeeper who raised a Japanese home appliance company with bare fists. He became interested in the founding Soka Gakkai International because he heard from his company employee about Buddhist ideology and the peace movement that the SGI was promoting.

With a strong interest in the Soka Gakkai International, which developed brilliantly in a short period of time, and the young leader of the SGI, Daisaku Ikeda, Matsushita attended the Tokyo Cultural Festival hosted by the SGI.

It was not long before the Cultural Festival began. When he saw the splendid yet unceasing performances of the producers and the changing human characters of the card section, he watched holding his breath. He marveled at the epic poetry of

Nietzscheanism is completed by SGI this way

unity, rarely seen in today's chaotic human society.

Matsushita later said this in his autobiography 「Q&A of Life」.

"First of all, I was impressed by the hospitality and kindness of the guides. We also tend to be very attentive when inviting important customers, but I felt that they are doing much more than we are.

From the moment I stepped into the hall, I was excited. With the grand and splendid card sections and acting going on, the entire hall turned into a place of one artwork. It was a dynamic art. It was the height of beauty beyond all description. I was moved. A wave of emotion did not let me lie still.

- Omit -

I was really impressed by the fact that I could do this kind of work today when society was in turmoil. And I could see the true value of the Soka Gakkai. I felt the human heart, the breadth and the depth of power, to do such a thing."

SGI President Ikeda did not have a chance to have a private conversation with Matsushita at the cultural festival. So he sent a few officials to thank Matsushita politely and asked if there were any inconveniences. "He must have been very busy with nearly 100,000 people gathered and thousands of people invited. I was very surprised at how much he cared about even that point. He really values people, and he respects them with all his heart."

Daisaku Ikeda has always cherished a one-time meeting with the desire to make everyone who has a relationship with him to the person who understands the SGI best.

"An encounter between a person and a person is 'a once in a lifetime'. A suggestion is a victory or defeat that needs sincerity. Failure is never allowed."

This was Ikeda's determination and conviction, who has been responsible for all the academic events since his youth.

The following year, Matsushita sent a message to Ikeda to meet him and hear from him. 'I will visit you wherever you are.' Coincidentally, however, Ikeda's schedule has been set for quite some time. It was inevitable that Matsushita would be invited to attend a ceremony to celebrate the cherry tree planting at headquarters on April 28.

Before the event began, Ikeda went to Matsushita, who was sitting at the meeting place, to say hello.

"I'm very sorry to have you take a long walk to Shizuoka."

Then Matsushita said, "Thank you very much for doing me a great favor and for taking the time," and thanked Ikeda with

Nietzscheanism is completed by SGI this way

such a gracious and respectful way. His sincerity was a shining attitude.

Ikeda and his wife, Kaneko, welcomed Matsushita's visit while drinking tea outside as the event ended, and soon moved indoors.

Matsushita worried that people's spirits were becoming dilapidated and goodwill was gradually disappearing.

"If we go this way, Japan will not develop."

Ikeda replied.

"I think so, too. Most people have become slaves to desire. It's because you only think about yourself. The basis for creating a good society is to transform ourselves. We call it 'the Human Revolution'. Each person must establish a solid philosophy of life and death, of human, of happiness, of space, of life and devote oneself to life. In fact, Buddhism is the philosophy of life, and it's the way of human revolution."

Matsushita was listening to Ikeda, his eyes shining, nodding his head. He listened to Ikeda with his back straightened out. He didn't even sit back comfortably. It looked like an old man who sought the law with a whole heart. Ikeda went on speaking in a grateful mind.

Their conversation was hardly ever ending. Since the two

have not had many opportunities to meet each other in person, they decided to exchange messages such as things they wanted to hear or topics they wanted to talk about.

Matsushita stepped down as chairman of Matsushita Electricity Industry in July that year and took charge of the company's advisor. He has been asking questions to President Ikeda repeatedly as if he had been waiting. It was all about Japan's serious direction of the future. Topics covered everything around the world such as politics and economy as well as human theory, life theory, and civilization. What to do for the 21st century was full of passion. There is a burning passion for those who live on the basis of responsibilities and mission. The joy of life and the joy of the lively motion waves.

Matsushita was about to be eighty years old. Ikeda was young enough to be less than fifty years old. So he thought, 'It's a duty for me to ask questions and be taught.' Ikeda paid great attention to asking questions. Even if he had a lot of questions, it could be rude to the other side if it is not a good question. A key question leads to a good answer, but a question that misses the point only makes the other party agonize and waste time.

Matsushita is a life's great senior. Therefore, he especially wanted to hear opinions about how humans should live. Ikeda's

Nietzscheanism is completed by SGI this way

question also became a fundamental question. The questions were like this. "What are the most humane conditions?" "What do you think of women's characters and roles?" "What do you need to live without regret in life?"

When Ikeda asked, "I want to hear the hardest thing you've ever done in your life." Then, Matsushita gave an unexpected answer.

"Actually, this is the hardest question to answer. Because when I look back quietly on my path, I don't feel very distressed or very hard in past. You may think it must have been very hard for others to see, but I didn't think I was suffering because I always saw a light of hope, a joy in the struggling."

And Matsushita went on like this.

"In my case, I just tried my best every day. And in the process, I always had hope, so I didn't think about hardship. I always work at the risk of my life."

It does not feel like a struggle for a person who fully burns himself and engages in the task he or she faced at that time. In other words, it could be called a "Welcomed Fight(歡鬪)".

Ikeda asked Matsushita for his opinion on 'Gratitude'

Matsushita considered 'Gratitude' the most important of life's guidelines or creed. He wrote the reason like this. "Appreciation and gratitude give us unlimited joy and vitality, and if these minds are strong, you can overcome any difficulties and they become the fundamentals of true happiness, and knowing the Gratitude is the most nourishing thing for a mind." Daisaku Ikeda was impressed.

As the answers to questions asked by Konosuke Matsushita by Daisaku Ikeda are almost finished in the letter, the editor of the magazine <Weekly Asahi> asked the disclosure of this conversation. Both Matsushita and Ikeda didn't intend to announce it publicly. However, both agreed as the editor enthusiastically urged them.

Their conversation was published in a two-volume book titled 『Q&A of Life』. in October of that year by Ushio publishing company.

Nietzscheanism is completed by SGI this way

Part 17

UCLA, invited lecture

President Ikeda headed for the lecture hall under the guidance of Vice President Miller. On the premises of UCLA, a prestigious university in Los Angeles, statues of renowned sculptors were everywhere including Rodin's 'The Thinker'. Listening to the vice-president's explanation, he wondered the excellent educational environment in which students could routinely deal with world-class works.

Outside the Dickson Hall which would be the place of lecture, a number of students had been waiting for President Ikeda's lecture for an hour. Daisaku Ikeda, the founder of Soka University and the Soka Gakkai International, representative Buddhist group of Japan, gathered by himself and herself after hearing that he was giving a lecture on the philosophy of life by the bulletin board of the University or University newspaper.

By the time Ikeda arrived at the lecture hall, about 600 people, including professors and students, were already filling the auditorium. On each side of the platform was decorated with large flowers and the big banner in English, 'A proposal for 21st-century, lecturer President Daisaku Ikeda' was hung at the back wall.

Ikeda began his historic university lecture on April 1 (1974) at 3 p.m. local time. It was 7 a.m. on April 2nd in Japanese time, which is the morning of the anniversary of his mentor, Josei Toda's death. While waiting for the lecture to begin, he vividly recalled the past when he was entrusted with Great propagation of Buddhism globally by Toda.

The Summer of 1954.

It happened when President Daisaku Ikeda visited Atsuda Village in the North Sea, his teacher's hometown, along with his former mentor, Josei Toda. Toda said, standing on the shore of Atsuda, watching the slowly surging waves.

"I will lay a rock-like foundation for the Great propagation of Buddhism in Japan. You need to clear the way for the world's Great propagation of Buddhism. I'll make a plan. I want you to

Nietzscheanism is completed by SGI this way

make it all happen."

Young Ikeda deeply kept the word of his teacher into his heart as if he were listening to his teacher's will. He believed that he could even risk his life for the propagation of the philosophy of dignity of life of Buddhism and the Peace thought of Buddhism.

Only when the student realizes his teacher's idea can he achieve the great wish of Great propagation of Buddhism. And there is a true 'way of teacher and student'.

President Ikeda spoke to Josei Toda in his mind at the Dickson Hall at UCLA.

Teacher! I came the to Los Angeles campus of the prestigious University of California in the United States today. From now on, on behalf of you, I will tell them the theory of life of Buddhism. I'm going to shout the idea of Soka Gakkai into the world. Please watch the student fight.'

Toda's face, smiling and nodding, rose from Ikeda's heart. Courage rose at the thought of the teacher. There was a flood of delight. That's true teacher and student.

Soon after, amid thunderous applause, President Ikeda began his lecture. His loud but warm voice rang out clearly in the auditorium.

"Today, I am very happy to be invited to speak on the campus of the UCLA, which represents the intelligence of the United States by the invitation of President Young and Vice-President Miller. I'm going to talk as the friend telling future instead of a lecturer, with infinite expectation and respect to you who will be in charge of the 21st century."

Ikeda first outlined his talks with British historian Dr. Arnold Toynbee last year. And the Doctor's warning was introduced as the following sentences.

"In the 20th century, mankind was intoxicated by the power of technology. But it eventually harmed the natural environment and brought about the self-destruction of mankind. Now mankind must acquire the wisdom to stare and control itself."

In the meeting between them, President Ikeda and Dr. Toynbee, have been in agreement that "The theory of looking at life with absolute dignity should be informed to mankind. So the whole human race can recognize 'the dignity of life' together.", and appealed to the audience like this.

"I think it is 'the century of life' to conclude the coming century. No, I believe it should be. That's because, in my opinion, that's the only way we can develop from technology civilization to humanity civilization truly."

Nietzscheanism is completed by SGI this way

Then he explained the life taught in Buddhism as birth, old age, sickness, and death, i.e., accumulation of suffering, and discussed why people feel pain in life.

Buddhism claims that it is because we are too obsessed with everything and its shape, which is truly vain and to become the prisoner of anguish.

Contemporary civilization has also developed on the basis of obsession, anguish, and fulfillment of this 'vain' things. As a result, although mankind has acquired convenience and comfort, it can be said that terrible threats, such as environmental destruction and nuclear war, are finally putting mankind into a swamp of destruction.

Some Buddhists teach that there is no other way but to sever the anguish to be free from the anguish. If so, can humans sever the anguish? Not really. As long as human beings are alive, it is natural human feelings to cling to life, to cherish love, and to seek benefits. The truth of the Buddhism is not that it should stop the anguish and abandon its obsession.

Being obsessed with agonies, played by the desire, and confused by vain phenomenon means that my oneself, as to say bind to 'the Little Self' The true Buddhism explains that there is an unchanging rule that makes them united and moves in a constant rule in the life that makes agony and obsession and in the vain reality.

And it is taught that realizing this universal truth and embracing vain phenomenon, that is to live as 'the Big Self'. This 'the Big Self' means 'Ubermensch' that Nietzsche talked, who is the fundamental power of the Universe which reveals various movements of life, is the 'law'. Doctor Toynbee described this as 'the ultimate reality' of the Universe.

Ikeda's topic was the ultimate philosophy of life, which is Buddhism, and it can be said that it is difficult. However, the professors and students who attended listened hard, glistening their eyes at his words explaining the secrets of the theory of life.

Furthermore, he said that standing in 'the Big Self' is not about abandoning 'the Small Self' but about controlling and surviving the 'the Small Self' for human well-being. If 'the Small Self' is compared to the fiercely running train, 'the Big Self' is the track on which the train is running. If the train is derailed it will be out of order and rollover, but if it goes into a certain track which is 'the Big Self', solid happiness can be got.

Ikeda then discussed life and death, which can be said to be the biggest topic in human life, in connection with 'the Big Self'.

Nietzscheanism is completed by SGI this way

"The Buddhism says 'life and death cannot be the two'." Both life and death are outwardly represented by the eternal flow of living, and neither of them is subordinate to the other. For example, humans change greatly both in body and mind after birth. But there's one thing about you that doesn't change consistently, which is oneself. Buddhism says that fundamental 'oneself' is connected to the life of scale of the Universe, as to say 'the Big Self'. This is the thinking method of 'life and death cannot be the two'. And human has 'the Big Self(Ubermensch, Buddha nature)' in the life of oneself.

Human life changes depending on what life and death he/she has. And furthermore, it determines the true nature of civilization. President Ikeda stressed that the civilization that has been dominated by 'the Small Self' should be transformed to the civilization which is breathing with 'the Big Self', which is the life of Universe, which is the reality of the vanity all the time.

His speech grew more heated as he moved on.

"The 21st century should be made into the 'century of life' when humans turn eyes to life. Whether or not the New Century is the civilization of the human dream depends on whether human finds the unchanging, i.e., firm, immobile, and strong life by a human."

And he ended the talk like the following words.

"A human being who is in danger of self-destruction due to his/her desire has not escaped the realm of intelligent animals in the extreme. In the scriptures of the great saint Nichiren, which I believe in, there is an expression of 'Beasts with talents'. Human should be human not only in intelligence but also be free from egoism and take a leap by oneself in life and mind."

"I found the way from Buddhism. And I started 'the Journey of Life'. I want you to think 'the way of human self-reliance', as a young constructor and pioneer entering an unheard transition era. If today's talk can serve as an indicator of your life, I would consider it a great honor. Thank you!"

His lecture, which lasted about one hour and fifteen minutes, was over.

The audience, packed tightly in the auditorium, stood up with a blush on their cheeks. And the next moment there was thunderous applause. Many people seemed to be moved freshly hearing the lecture. Some of them were stunned by the first encounter of Eastern wisdom and Buddhist thoughts and looked blank for a while.

Sunshine of life which eliminates the dark cloud of modern

civilization is the Buddhism, which is the law of life.

The UCLA lecture, which was Ikeda's first overseas lecture, ended in great success. He left the campus behind, drawing his teacher, Josei Toda, in the car, and prayed the things to be dealt of deep gratitude. When arriving at the hotel, President Ikeda told an accompanying official like this.

"To promulgate Buddhism to the society, we need to go and give lectures for Universities. Maybe someday I can give my lecture at Harvard University, don't I?"

No one imagined that his words would come true at this time. Later, however, President Ikeda gives lectures at the hall of world intellectuals such as Moscow University, Beijing University, the French Institute and Harvard University (two times) continuously.

Part 18

Harvard University, invited lecture

In this clean, fine weather, today at Harvard University, the best tradition in the United States, it is my honor to be invited again subsequently after 2 years, and I would like to express my deepest gratitude to you, including Professor Yaman, Professor Cox, Honorary Professor Galbraith.

The Greek philosopher Heracleitos left the famous saying, 'Everything is hereditary(panta rhei)'. Clearly, everything, whether it's human or natural world, is a continuity of change, and nothing stays the same for a moment. No solid gold stone cannot escape the abrasion of the earth in terms of the long term.

Even the remarkable transformation of human society is as the situation we are watching like panoramas in front of our

Nietzscheanism is completed by SGI this way

eyes, living at the end of 20th century, which is called 'Century of War and Revolution'

The Buddhist eye has captured the reality of this change as 'Various phenomena are changing all the time(諸行無常)'. Saying this in the view of the Universe, which is to say one world is to form, be inherited, and collapse for being the next formation.(成住壞空)

And if you think about this in terms of the view of life, anyone can't avoid the thought of birth, old age, sickness, and death, the four agonies of life, which is inherited.

This four agonies of life, especially the death, which means who has the life must die, was the reason for every religion or philosophy form the old days.

The episode of 'exiting four gates(四門出遊)', which is the reason of Sakyamuni's leaving home or the word of Plato, calling philosophy as 'Study of death are so famous, and the great saint Nichiren(日蓮) is also saying "Firstly, you need to learn things regarding death, and then you will learn other things."

Also, I had discussions through several days regarding various topics with extraordinary Historian Doctor Toynbee.

Why does death mean so much to humans, and it is because, above all, death brings us to the realization of our own finitude. No matter how rich or powerful a human is, he or she cannot escape the fate of dying one day. To recognize this finitude and overcome the fear or anxiety of death, humans can transcend the way of life of an animal instinct, by participating in some kind of eternity. That's why religion has been with human history for a long time.

But in the modern era, which is called the "Civilization of forgotten death," we've taken our eyes out of this fundamental task of life and took death into the position to be avoided like criminals.

For modern people, death is just a vacuum in the absence of a simple life, and if life is good, death is evil, life is existence, death is void, life is logic, death is illogic, life is the brightness, and death is darkness, and as I just said death had the image of minus until now.

As the result, modern people are now in severe revenge by death. As the word of Doctor Brzezinski, this century became 'the century of megadeath' as a result of 'the civilization forgot the death' ironically.

In recent years, the high interest of brain death, dignity death,

Nietzscheanism is completed by SGI this way

hospice, ideal funeral, and the study of 'Near death Medicine' by Madame Cubra Ross, in my opinion, means that everyone needs to review the meaning of death inevitably. Now it seems that modern civilization is just about to straighten out a great illusion.

Death is not just a lack of life, it's an integral part in parallel with life. The whole thing is 'life' and 'culture' as a way of life. So I think the biggest task of 21 century is the establishment of right values of life, values of life and death, and values of culture not excluding death, but staring death.

Buddhism says the image of life itself which is in the deep base of the phenomenon. And the whole thought is connected to appear, and it ceases to exist and continues the heredity.

Therefore, death is like the charging period, as human reserves vitality toward tomorrow by sleeping, death is not the thing to be avoided but like life, it needs to be regarded as benefit and pleasure.

So, Lotus Sutra, the essence of scriptures of Mahayana Buddhism, called the purpose of endlessly changing life as 'the life exists for joy(衆生所遊樂)', and it means as the degree of faith, life is delight, death is delight, life is amusement, and death is amusement. The great saint Nichiren also asserted 'It is a great delight of delights'.

The tragedy of 'the century of war and revolution' clearly left a lesson that the decisive factor in human happiness and unhappiness is not in the transformation of appearance alone. So in the next century, I'm sure that this transformation of values of life and death will be the most important task.

And I want to summarize the three points that I think will contribute to the civilization of the 21st century.

Firstly, it's called 'the source of peace'.

Perhaps the biggest reason why Buddhism has been colored as an image of peace from old times is that it has excluded violence and generally placed great importance on dialogue and the media.

Jaspers accurately assessed the sorrow of disciples who are mourning the death of Sakyamuni as 'We lost a man who used language freely'. In one scripture of Buddhism, calling Sakyamuni as 'the person who dealt with people with joy, without making a wry face, and talking to people firstly', and his whole life is a fulfillment of 'open conversation' by 'open mind' liberated from every bit of dogma.

Nietzscheanism is completed by SGI this way

Scripture of Buddhism of the final trip of Sakyamuni who was at the old age of 80, starts from the episode which is about stopping the will to the war by the persuasion of media. In other words, not by directly advising the Magada, high official of the great country of hegemonism, which is trying to conquer neighboring country Vrijji, but by saying the duty of the country's rise and decline exquisitely avoided invasion undoubtedly.

In addition, the final chapter of this scripture of Buddhism describes a touching scene in which Sakyamuni, near his deathbed, talks about law and asceticism, and recommends two or three times of conversation to ensure that no regrets are left. The beginning and the end of the last journey of Sakyamuni highlighted the sparkle of media like this and vividly revealing the face of 'man who used language freely'.

Why was Sakyamuni so free in conversation? It is because an enlightened man's broad respect and affection were free from dogma, prejudice, or obsession. Sakyamuni once said, "I saw an arrow stuck in humans' mind.".

This "arrow" could be termed the arrow of a discriminatory consciousness, an unreasoning emphasis on difference.

Nietzsche and Ikeda

The India of his time was in a period of transition and upheaval, in which the horrors of conflict and war were an ever-present reality. To Shakyamuni's penetrating gaze, it was clear that the underlying cause of this conflict was an attachment to differences such as those of ethnicity and nationality.

Speaking in the early years of this century, Josiah Royce, one of many important philosophers Harvard has given the world, declared as follows: "Reform, in such matters, must come, if at all, from within . . . The public as a whole is whatever the processes that occur, for good or evil, in individual minds, may determine."

Indeed, the "invisible arrow" of evil to be overcome is not to be found in races and classes external to ourselves but embodied in our own heart. The conquest of our own prejudicial thinking, our own attachment to the difference, is the guiding principle for open dialogue, the essential condition for the establishment of peace and universal respect for human rights.

It was his own complete release from the prejudice that enabled Shakyamuni to expound the Law with such freedom, adapting his style of teaching to the character and capacity of his interlocutor.

Nietzscheanism is completed by SGI this way

Whether mediating a communal dispute over water-rights, converting a violent criminal, or admonishing one who objected to the practice of begging for alms, the quality we find throughout Shakyamuni's dialogues is the effort to make others aware of the "arrow" of their inner evil.

It was the power of his extraordinary character that brought these words to the lips of one contemporaneous sovereign: "Those whom we, with weapons, cannot force to surrender, you subdue unarmed."

Only through overcoming attachment to difference can a religion rise above an essentially tribal outlook to offer a global faith.

When, for example, Nichiren dismisses the Japanese Shogunate authorities who were persecuting him as the "rulers of this little island country" it is clear that his vision was directed toward a world religion embodying universal values, transcending the confines of a single state.

It should also be noted that dialogue is not limited to the kind of placid exchanges that might be likened to the wafting of a spring breeze. There are times when to break the grip arrogance has on another, speech must be like the breath of fire. In my opinion, in the true conversation opposition is one expression of unity.

When I met professor Yaman and professor Sullivan, I said that the conversation is the most important task because of this reason.

Formerly professor Yaman already introduced, our Soka Gakkai International challenged head-on the forces of Japanese militarism during World War II. As a result, many members, beginning with founder and first president Tsunesaburo Makiguchi, were imprisoned. It was exactly 50 years from now.

First President Makiguchi died in his age of 73 in prison with explaining even his guards and interrogators the principles of Buddhism and peace. Heir to Makiguchi's spiritual legacy, second president Josei Toda emerged from the ordeal of 'a two-year imprisonment' and, declaring his faith in 'the global human family', engaged in widespread dialogue among the suffering common people.

The second point I would like to touch upon is the role that Buddhism can play in 'the restoration of humanity, the rejuvenation of the human person'.

In an age marked by a widespread religious revival, we need always to ask: Does religion make people stronger, or does it

Nietzscheanism is completed by SGI this way

weaken them? Does it encourage what is good or what is evil in them? Are they made better and wiser--or less--by religion? These, I believe, are the criteria we must keep firmly in view.

While the authority of Marx as a social prophet has been largely undermined by the collapse of socialism in eastern Europe and the former Soviet Union, there is an important truth contained in his equating of religion to opium.

And although one hopes that the recent tragedy in Waco, Texas, represents a rare extremity, it is not clear that all religions have rid themselves of their opiate-like aspects. In fact, there is a reason for concern that more than a few of the religions finding new life in the twilight of this century are characterized by dogmatism and insularity that run counter to the accelerating trend toward interdependence and cross-cultural interaction.

In this regard, it is important to examine the balance different belief-systems accord to reliance on our own powers and reliance on powers external to ourselves, ideas corresponding roughly to free will and grace in Christian terminology.

If we paint in the broadest strokes the movement from the medieval to the modern in Europe, we observe steady progress away from a God-centered determinism, toward an ever greater emphasis on free will and human responsibility.

The powers of the human being have increasingly been stressed, while those external to us have been steadily de-emphasized.

And while none would deny the great achievements of science and technology in the modern era, a misplaced faith in the omnipotence of reason has led humanity to believe that there is nothing beyond our power, thus bringing civilization to its present, apparently inextricable impasse.

If past reliance on an external force led humanity to underestimate the full dimensions of our possibility and responsibility, excessive faith in our own powers has produced a dangerous overinflation of the human ego.

Could it not be said that civilization is now seeking a third path, a new balance between faith in our own power and recognition of that which lies beyond us.

In that point, Mahayana Buddhism said, "Neither solely through one's own efforts . . . nor solely through the power of others.", and suggests an excellent balance between these two forces.

Furthermore, Dewey advocated 'faith by everyone' and appealed the indispensability of 'the religious thing' rather than a certain religion.

Nietzscheanism is completed by SGI this way

It is because the religion can easily lead people to the self-righteousness or fanaticism, but 'the religious thing' unites human interest and energy, and leads the activity and stimulates emotion and generate the light of intelligence, and it can generate and enlighten every art, knowledge, effort, resting after working, intimate exchange and education, friendship and romance, and the growth of faith.

While Dewey does not identify a specific external power, for him "the religious" is a generalized term for that which supports and encourages people in active aspiration toward the good and the valuable.

'The religious' means helping those who help themselves.

As the results of modern man's self-worship make sadly evident, unassisted we are incapable of realizing our full potential. It is only through fusing and merging ourselves with the eternal--that which lies beyond our finitude as individuals--that we can manifest the full scale of our potential.

And yet that potential(By Editor: in this context, it means the power of Buddhism) is not foreign to us, but is of us, within us, and always has been. Such, I believe, are the implications of Dewey's argument. Further, I believe that the balance each religious tradition strikes between inner and exterior forces will decisively influence that tradition's future viability.

Not only Buddhists but all involved in religion must devote careful attention to this relationship if we are to avoid repeating the history of human enslavement to dogma and religious authority and assure that the religious impulse serves as a vehicle for the restoration and rejuvenation of humanity.

Thank you for the saying that our Soka Gakkai International's activity suggests 'the direction of humanism religion' by professor Cox with a close look.

The third point I would like to discuss is the philosophical basis which Buddhism provides for 'the symbiotic coexistence of all things'.

Among the many images in Lotus Sutra, one that I find particularly compelling is that of an impartial rain that compassionately moistens the vast expanse of the earth, bringing forth new life from all the trees and grasses, large and small.

This scene, depicted with a vividness, grandeur and beauty characteristic of the Lotus Sutra, symbolizes the enlightenment of all people touched by the Buddha's Law of great and impartial wisdom. At the same time, it is a magnificent paean

Nietzscheanism is completed by SGI this way

to the rich diversity of human as well as all forms of sentient and insentient life, each equally manifesting the inherent enlightenment of its nature, each thriving and harmonizing in 'a grand concert of symbiosis'.

As you know, Buddhism uses the term 'dependent origination' to describe symbiotic relations. Nothing--no one--exists in isolation. Each individual existence functions to bring into being the environment which in turn sustains all other existences.

All things, mutually supportive and related, form a living cosmos, what modem philosophy might term a semantic whole. This is the conceptual framework through which Mahayana Buddhism views the natural universe.

Speaking through Faust, Goethe gives voice to a similar vision. 'All weaves one fabric; all things give/Power unto all to work and live."

The poet, whose insights now strike us for their remarkable affinity to Buddhism, was criticized by his young friend Eckermann as "lacking confirmation of his presentiments." The intervening years have offered a steadily swelling chorus of affirmation for the prescience of Goethe's, and Buddhism's, deductive vision.

Taking as an example the concept of causation, we find that causal relations viewed in the light of dependent origination differ fundamentally from the kind of mechanistic causation which, according to modern science, holds sway over the objective natural world--a world divorced from subjective human concerns. Causation, in the Buddhist view, spans a more broadly defined nature, one that embraces human existence.

To illustrate, let us assume that an accident or disaster has occurred.

A mechanistic theory of causation can be used to pursue and identify how the accident occurred but is silent regarding the question of why certain individuals should find themselves caught up in the tragic event. Indeed, the mechanistic view of nature requires the deliberate forestalling of such existential questionings.

In contrast, the Buddhist understanding of causation seeks to directly address these poignant "whys?", as demonstrated by this question and response early in Shakyamuni's career: "What is the cause of aging and death? Birth is the cause of aging and death.".

In a later era, through a process of exhaustive thought and inquiry, the founder of the Chinese T'ien T'ai school, Chih-i, developed a theoretical structure, comprising such concepts as the 'three thousand realms in a single life-moment' which is not only sweeping in scope and rigorous in elaboration but is entirely compatible with modern science.

While limitations of time prohibit elaboration, it is worth mentioning that many contemporary fields of inquiry--among them ecology, transpersonal psychology, and quantum mechanics--are remarkably cognate with Buddhism in their approach and conclusions.

In the scriptures of Buddhism, there are saying like this. "You are your own master. Could anyone else be your master? When you have gained control over your self, you have found a master of rare value." and "Be lamps unto yourselves. Rely on yourselves. Hold fast to the Law as a lamp, do not rely on anything else."

Both passages urge us to live independently, true to ourselves and unswayed by others.

The "self" referred to here, however, is not what Buddhism terms the "the small self", caught up in the snares of egoism. Rather, it is the "the big self(Ubermensch)" fused with the universal life through which cause and effect intertwine over the infinite reaches of space and time.

'The great self' is profoundly resonant with the unifying and integrating "self" which Jung perceived in the depths of the ego, and with what Emerson spoke of as "the universal beauty, to which every part and particle is equally related; the eternal One." I am firmly convinced that a wide-scale awakening to this greater self will give rise to a world of creative and symbiotic coexistence in the coming century.

'The big self' taught in Mahayana Buddhism is always spreading the activity of lessening agony and giving delight toward people of real society, and it is the other name of 'open personality' which is making every human's agony to one's agony.

By forming this great solidarity of humanity(By Editor: the superhuman life that Nietzsche taught), the prospect of a new civilization which is breaking through the blockade of so-called 'modern ego' may exist. Also, the great human character is to be established in the pulsation of dynamic big self on the values of life and death, saying "Life is joy and death is joy, too."

In the record of his 「orally transmitted holy teachings」, Nichiren states that "We adorn the treasure tower of our being with the four aspects [of birth, aging, sickness, and death]."

Nietzscheanism is completed by SGI this way

It is my earnest desire and prayer that in the twenty-first century each member of the human family will bring forth the natural luster of this inner 'treasure tower of life' and, wrapping our azure planet in the symphonic tones of 'open dialogue', humankind will make its evolutionary advance into 'the third millennium'.

Sharing with you this vista--of the brilliant dawn of a century of peace and humanity--I conclude my remarks.

Thank you very much for listening.

Epilogue

Udumbara is the legendary flower tree in imagination. It is known that if this flower blooms, the Buddha will appear, and at the time of the Buddha's appearance, and it is compared to reuniting Buddha can be really hard.

There was a strange rumor. It is there are people who saw Udumbara, or who could smell the scent of the flower. The more astonishing truth was that a rumor from the Soka Gakkai International in Japan.

The SGI which has been established to contribute to the human society and the stories of a believer living as a member of SGI were decorated through Nietzsche and Ikeda to furnish this book.

By the way, Nietzscheanism which is called as 'the flower

of the modern philosophy' had an honorable role to fire up the 'Soka Renaissance'. The writer says regarding the way of practicing asceticism which Nietzsche was sad about because he didn't finalize, latter SGI President Ikeda proved the greatness of the way of practicing asceticism instead of Nietzsche."

Lotus Sutra by Buddha was not correctly given. It was the SGI that discovered 'the truth of Lotus Sutra', and according to Nichiren's Buddhism scriptures, that timing was exactly 3,000 years from the talking of Buddha about Lotus Sutra.

What Nietzsche told about 'the way to become superhuman', Ubermensch is well known and already generalized in SGI(Soka Gakkai International) long ago.

The writer hopes that about two important matters, discovering 'the truth of Lotus Sutra' and 'the way to become superhuman' will be finished by future scholars.

I think every person has a life story of oneself in one's mind. Among them, there were several people who wrote it as a biography. Frankly, I admire them when I meet them.

It is hard to say what kind of life is great and valuable. However, if I receive that kind of question, I'd like to say like this. "Isn't it the life which burns oneself until the last moment of life?"

In my latter years, I wanted to sort the stories of my life into one book. Among them the 3 Presidents' lives which already become the part of my life, I wanted to describe their table of contents' life stories as episodes, and to say to others.

I didn't have many friends, but publishing this book will help to have a conversation with a diverse spectrum's people, and developing friendships. Conversation connects to human and broadens the wave of resonance to the friendship. And that friendship gathers to color our life more fertile.

I hope the readers' warm support.

From Los Angeles
Charles Lee

Publication Rights

Printing the first edition on May 26th, 2019
Publishing the 2nd edition on May 17th, 2019
Author Charles Lee
Publisher Kim Yang-soo

Publishing by Publishing Group Pure Fountain
Publishing Registration 2012-000035
Address Seo-hyun plaza 604, Jungang-ro 1456(Joo-yeop dong), Ilsanseo-gu, Goyang-si, Gyeonggi-do, Republic of Korea
Phone 031) 906-5006
Fax 031) 906-5079
Homepage www.booksam.kr
Email okbook1234@naver.com
ISBN 979-11-5778-369-4 (03800)